INTRODUCTION
TO
JEWELRY CASTING

OTHER HOBBY BOOKS IN THIS SERIES INCLUDE:

Jewelry Making as a Hobby
Clock Repairing as a Hobby
Watch Repairing as a Hobby
Finding and Preparing Precious and Semiprecious Stones

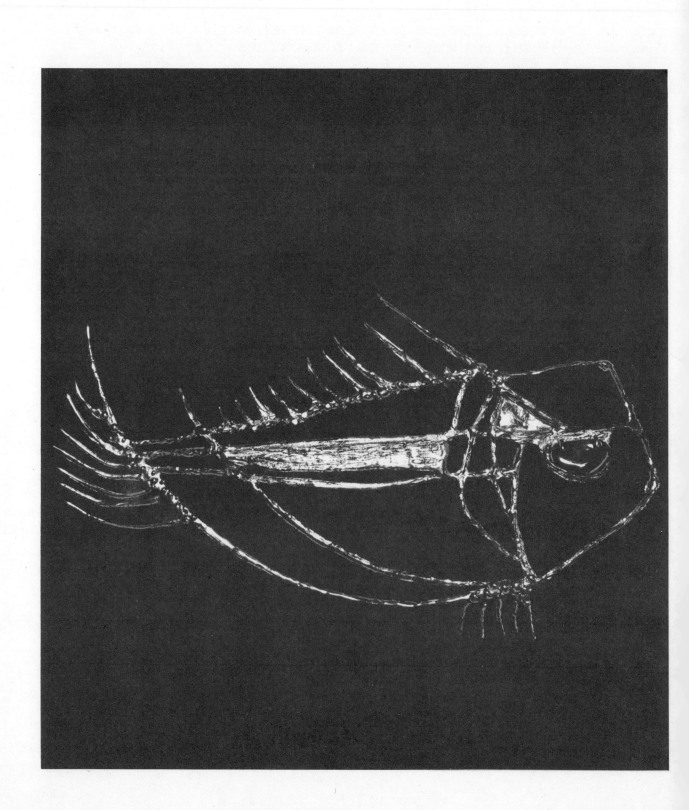

INTRODUCTION TO JEWELRY CASTING

An Illustrated Guide to Casting Methods for the
Beginning Craftsman and Hobbyist

ROBERT WALD

ASSOCIATION PRESS ■ NEW YORK

INTRODUCTION TO JEWELRY CASTING

Copyright © 1975 by Robert Wald

Association Press, 291 Broadway, New York, N.Y. 10007

The photographs in Chapter 11 were contributed by the respective craftsmen. Figures 26, 94, 98, 108, and 110 were contributed by Abbey Materials Corp., while Figures 108A, 109, and 111 are from B. Jadow and Sons. The remainder are by the Author.

International Standard Book Number: 0-8096-1885-0

Library of Congress Cataloging in Publication Data

Wald, Robert.
Introduction to jewelry casting

1. Jewelry making—Amateurs' manuals. 2. Precision casting—Amateurs' manuals. I. Title.
TT212.W34   745.59'42   74-18098
ISBN 0-8096-1885-0

Printed in the United States of America
Designed by The Etheredges

To

Marjorie, Diane, Jan David,

Jerry and Tina

CONTENTS

INTRODUCTION
TO
JEWELRY CASTING

TO THE READER: A PREVIEW

If you are interested in creating distinctive jewelry by one or more of a number of casting techniques, then you could, with the help of this book, soon be on your way to becoming involved in one of the most exciting, challenging and rewarding forms of art and craft work you can possibly imagine. A great advantage of jewelry casting is that you can fashion one-of-a-kind rings, brooches, pendants, necklaces, bracelets, cuff links, tie-tacks and other fine body ornaments—ranging from the simple to the exotic—which cannot be made in any other way. Casting jewelry is, in the main, considerably easier than the other basic method of constructing it from metal sheet and wire. The applications are broad and flexible, and include a good selection of metals in which the objects can be cast. Moreover, should you not like the article that you cast, you can remelt the metal and use it in another casting. There is little wasted metal in casting jewelry.

Another outstanding advantage of crafting jewelry by the casting process is that you can become a designer/craftsman with only a small outlay of money. On the other hand, if your pocketbook can afford it, you can invest as much as you wish in equipment that is fascinating to work with and which will enlarge your creative horizon. Once you learn certain procedures, you can cast not only jewelry but also chess pieces for a chess set, fishing lures, small sculpture, parts for model ships, cars or airplanes, as well as dozens of other items.

The art of jewelry casting is within the capability of all who can read simple instructions and apply them intelligently. It is a craft that can easily be learned by the teen-ager, the senior citizen and others in between. It offers an excellent opportunity to those who are searching for a way to use their leisuretime creatively and productively, and the craft also has excellent therapeutic benefits. As for those who will say: "How can I design a piece of jewelry? I'm no artist. I can't even draw a straight line!", there are obvious answers. First, with the help of a straightedge, anyone can draw a straight line. Moreover, a curved or wavy line has much more eye appeal and artistic individuality than a straight line. This is not to imply that it does not take a certain amount of patience and practice to acquire skill in jewelry casting, for it does. But if you are willing to devote enough time and effort to learning the basic steps, you will be astonished and delighted at the knowledge and know-how you can achieve in a short period of time. Here is hoping that you will try. For, in the author's honest opinion, you will not just like it, you will love it!

The purpose of this book is to provide the novice (or teachers of the craft) with an easy-to-follow, step-by-step text that describes in simple language how jewelry can be cast using any one of several different procedures. The book has been written with the thought that beginners, working alone, should be able to attain the skill needed to create pieces of jewelry that will satisfy their creative urge. Some of the chapters show and explain how the author made a specific item of jewelry. The purpose is not to have students duplicate the item but to give them some notion of what techniques must be practiced in order to gain experience. It is sincerely hoped that once newcomers are familiar with the basic processes, they will go on to designing their own articles with the help of their own ingenuity and imagination. It is also hoped that experienced craftsmen who have not tried casting will find the book a useful introduction to this method of jewelry making, and that if they have tried their hand at it, they may find in this book an approach they have not yet explored.

The book starts with a creative procedure that all newcomers to the field of jewelry casting can do, and do well. It is called "drop casting," and, as far as the author can determine, is a fairly modern technique that lends itself admirably to the contemporary taste for free-form jewelry. It is a technique that acquaints the novice with the handling of molten metal, that requires only a few fairly inexpensive tools and supplies to achieve unusual and individual articles of jewelry, and that should give the novice a sense of accomplishment right from the outset. Next, there is the casting of jewelry using cuttlefish bones, another easily mastered technique. Here, the beginner learns to create his own models in wax. The major portion of the book, however, is devoted to demonstrating and explaining the lost wax process, which is the one most craftsmen who cast jewelry employ today. The text discusses the variety of waxes that can be used, the prime methods by which wax models are constructed and designed, the investment and burnout procedures and the types of equipment, including the inexpensive, utilized in casting jewelry by the lost wax process.

In an appendix, the reader will find a list of suppliers who sell everything needed for casting jewelry by any method. It is earnestly recommended that the beginner send for the catalogs these concerns offer; for in these he will find information that supplements this text that space did not permit including here. Some suppliers send their catalogs free, some charge a modest amount that in many cases is refundable upon the first small purchase from the supplier.

Finally, it should be noted that in using this book newcomers to jewelry casting are expected to have at least a working knowledge of the main jewelry-making processes such as sawing, filing, soldering (especially with hard solder), annealing, pickling, polishing and coloring of the craft metals, plus the small amount of equipment and supplies required to perform these operations. Space does not permit the demonstration and explanation of these techniques which alone can fill a book as they did in the author's *Jewelry Making as a Hobby*. Reading a good text—along with some diligent practice—will enable the beginner to get started in jewelry casting . . . as we will do right after the author thanks those who helped him in the preparation of this book.

The author thanks the Abbey Materials Corporation of New York City for the photographic and other assistance given in support of the text and Thomas DeLeo of that firm for his continuing interest in the book's development. I also appreciate the patient encouragement of Anthony Lalley of the William Dixon Company and the editorial counsel and guidance of Robert Roy Wright of Association Press. Special thanks go to the master craftsmen for permitting me to exhibit the excellence and diversity of their creative efforts.

Chapter One

DROP CASTING

THE METALS USED IN CASTING

Before going into the how-to of drop casting, a brief word must be said about the metals that are most suitable for jewelry casting. This selection is based on the fact that some craft metals have characteristics that make them unsuitable for casting (*e.g.,* copper) or are not worth the trouble (*e.g.,* nickel silver, aluminum). Pure gold and pure silver are not included because they are too soft for most jewelry purposes. Others have been excluded because the heating equipment used by most craftsmen cannot attain the high temperatures required to melt certain metals. Platinum and platinum alloys, for example, melt at temperatures of 3,000 degrees Fahrenheit and over. (*Note:* From this point on, it should be understood that all temperatures will be given in Fahrenheit readings.) The platinum family of metals is widely used by commercial jewelers who have the equipment to produce these temperatures, but individual craftsmen, as a rule, do not. Most noncommercial torches can handle metals with a melting point of 2,000 to 2,400 degrees. When one adds the extremely high cost of the platinum metals to the melting temperatures required, it is understandable that very few craftsmen use these metals for casting or even for constructing jewelry.

Listed below, along with their melting points, are the metals most often used by one-of-a-kind jewelry casters. Pewter and brass are listed because they are relatively inexpensive and make good practice metals. While pewter is too soft for most jewelry that gets a lot of wear (such as rings, bracelets, cuff links and the like), its resemblance to sterling silver, color-wise, should keep it from being ruled out completely for jewelry such as pendants and brooches.

Commercial manufacturers of costume jewelry use brass in many of their products, but it should be remembered that brass can cause a discoloration on the skin of some people. Bronze is included because of its low cost and because the kind sold by jewelry supply houses has a color that closely resembles gold.

TABLE I
METALS USED IN JEWELRY CASTING

METAL	MELTING POINT	METAL	MELTING POINT
Gold—18K		Gold—10K	
yellow	1700°	yellow	1665°
white	1730°	white	1975°
red	1655°	red	1765°
green	1810°	green	1580°
—14K			
yellow	1615°	Sterling silver	1640°
white	1825°	Bronze	1825°
red	1715°	Brass	930°
green	1765°	Pewter	440°

For all methods of casting, the gold in the above karats and colors and sterling silver (from here on referred to only as silver) can be bought in grains (pellets) the size of peas. The cost is usually a little less than for sheet and wire which require more labor than grains to produce in the proper gauges and shapes. If grains are not available, sheet and wire can be cut into small pieces (*e.g.*, sheet ½ in. square, wire 1 in. long). Scrap pieces of metal cut from jewelry previously constructed or from what was previously cast can also be used. Brass and pewter are only available in circles, sheet and wire. Bronze is also obtainable in sheet and wire, but some suppliers offer small bars of bronze from which small pieces can be cut with a jeweler's saw or hacksaw. Brass, pewter and bronze sheet and wire should be cut into the same sizes as suggested above for gold and silver.

WHAT YOU NEED

The possibilities for making very different, one-of-a-kind jewelry by the drop-casting method are virtually unlimited. The list of materials and equipment needed for drop casting is not long, and it may be comforting to know that if you must buy some of the items listed below, most of them are also used in other methods of casting.

1. A supply of metal to be cast, of course.

Figure 1.
Earthenware crock.

2. A torch with which to melt the metal—a propane torch, a Prest-O-Lite or any other that will provide the necessary amount of heat.

3. A metal pail, metal pot or earthenware crock deep enough to hold three to four inches of water, ice cubes or cracked ice, and still have room above to act as a splash shield when the hot metal is dropped into it (see Figure 1). Plastic pails or teflon-coated pots should be avoided since the heated metal will burn through the plastic and teflon. Neither should glass, including Pyrex, utensils be used because the metal striking any part of their surface will produce cracks.

4. Flux to clean the metal and remove oxides as it is being melted. Ordinary powdered borax mixed half and half with boric acid or borax crystals alone will serve with all the casting metals except pewter, which does not require a flux for casting. Powdered borax is available usually where household cleaning products are sold; boric acid and borax crystals are obtainable from pharmacies.

5. Melting dish, casting crucible (the one-troy-ounce size, at least) or charcoal block available from jewelry supply companies (see Figure 2). If you plan to cast pewter as well as other metals, using a melting dish or crucible, it is well to have a separate one for pewter, for some of this metal may remain in the dish or crucible and ruin castings made from other metals. It is also advisable to melt one of the fluxes over the surface of the dish or crucible (including its top portion or cover). This serves as a sort of "glue" that keeps the refractory material of the dish or crucible from dusting or flaking off and ruining the casting. As shown in Figure 3, it is also a good idea to line the dish or crucible with 1/16-in. asbestos paper each time you cast a different metal. Even with asbestos linings, small particles of every metal have a way of staying behind when cast. They can then spoil a casting because they may not properly alloy or mix with another metal. Cut the asbestos paper to fit, dampen it with water and press it with your fingers so that it conforms to the shape of the dish or crucible. The paper will burn through after one or two castings so that you will have to renew it occasionally even if you are melting the same metal. If you use a charcoal block, carve a hemispheric

Figure 2. Melting dishes,
crucible, and charcoal block.

Figure 3. Asbestos paper makes
good lining for melting dish or crucible.

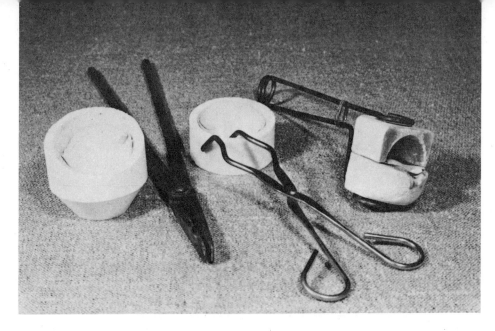

Figure 4. Common types of tongs.

depression in its center with a sharp knife into which you can deposit the metal to be cast. Then cut a funnel or spillway from the depression to one of the block's shorter sides. This will help in running the molten metal off the block. If you use a charcoal block for drop casting and change from one metal to another make sure that none of the previous metal remains behind.

6. Some type of tong is needed to lift and tilt the dish or crucible in casting the molten metal. Several different tongs are shown in Figure 4. As shown, special tongs are available for holding casting crucibles. These tongs have pointed prongs which grip the top and bottom of the crucible, and are secured to the crucible by tieing binding wire around them. Also, the charcoal block can be tied with binding wire to an ordinary kitchen spatula for safe handling (see Figure 5).

7. Asbestos gloves are useful where great heat must be handled. These may be optional for drop casting, but they are essential with other forms of casting. The author believes the gloves with fingers are less cumbersome than the mitt type.

8. An asbestos block 12 in. x 12 in. x ½ in. on which to place the melting dish, crucible or charcoal block when melting the metal and for other jewelry construction and casting processes is essential.

Figure 5. Charcoal block on spatula.

Figure 6.
Indicative of the
variety of
drop-cast forms.

THE HOW-TO OF DROP CASTING

Of first importance in drop casting is to make certain the metal you use is clean. If you are using tiny pieces of scrap metal in whole or in part, it is well to run a magnet through them to pick up any saw blade or file fragments that may be mixed in with the scrap. You should heat all the metal you are using with your torch just enough to burn away any dust, oil, grease, lint or other contaminants (be careful with pewter because of its low melting point). Pickle the metal (except pewter) and rinse in clear water. Pewter should be washed first in warm water and detergent to which a little household ammonia has been added, and then rinsed in clear water.

The next step is to decide what you will drop the molten metal into: water at room temperature? cold water? ice water? crushed ice? ice cubes? Part of the fun and excitement of drop casting is that the process lends itself to a great amount of experimentation. No one can tell another person precisely how to drop molten metal in order to cast specific forms. The forms (see Figure 6) will vary with (1) the temperature of the substance the metal is dropped into, (2) the metal used, (3) the amount melted and dropped in at one time, (4) the height from which the metal is dropped, and (5) with whether it is dropped quickly, less quickly, or slowly dribbled from its container. The thing to do is to experiment. And it is economical to do so, because, if you do not like any or all of the forms you get, you can remelt the metal (be sure to include all the tiny bits and pieces) and cast again.

To cast, place the metal in whatever container you are using to melt it in. Do not use more metal than your torch can melt in a minute or two, particularly bronze with its high melting point. Dust a pinch of flux over the metal (except pewter) with your fingers, a spatula or a teaspoon and apply heat. The metal is completely molten if it rolls whenever it is shaken a bit in its container. Sprinkle a little more flux on the molten metal. Raise the dish, crucible or charcoal block, keeping the torch flame on the metal, and cast. Mentally note the height at which the drop was made and how fast or slow the pour was made, so that if you like the results, you can repeat the operation with more of the same metal.

Remove the castings from the water or ice and examine them. Some may have sharp points or edges that can be removed, if you plan to use them, with a saw, file and sanding cloth. Some may be long and slender, but still may be usable in some way. One or two may be large and clumsy looking, but perhaps they may be cut apart, filed and sanded to make more interesting pieces. Or perhaps one looks like a small sculpture. Often a coppery gold color appears on silver castings. This is due to the copper in the alloy which somehow rises to the surface and tints it. Further heating and pickling will remove the color.

You have now reached the other part of the fun and fascination of drop casting, which involves studying the castings and letting your imagination suggest the jewelry that can be made from them. A single piece may be large enough to make a brooch or pendant. Perhaps there are two forms enough alike in shape and size to make a pair of earrings or cuff links. Move the pieces around and in juxtaposition to each other, bearing in mind that a different technique can be employed to fashion jewelry from the castings:

1. Smaller forms can be soldered together with hard solder to make larger forms. With pewter, use only soft solder and soft solder flux or the special pewter solders and pewter flux that are available. In Figure 7, silver castings were soldered together to make the brooch. The same was done with drop castings to create the pendant.

2. Prongs or even bezels can be soldered on to one or more pieces to provide a setting for one or more gemstones. Pearls can also be mounted to add still another decorative touch.

3. Jump rings can be soldered on the castings to make them part of a chain, necklace or bracelet. This was done in creating the silver chain for a pendant as shown in Figure 8.

4. Small forms of all metals except pewter can be *fused* together to make a larger and perhaps more interesting form. To fuse those metals that can be fused, place the pieces so that they touch or overlap one another;

Figure 7. Brooch and pendant were made from silver drop castings.

Figure 8. Silver chain was made by soldering jump rings on drop castings.

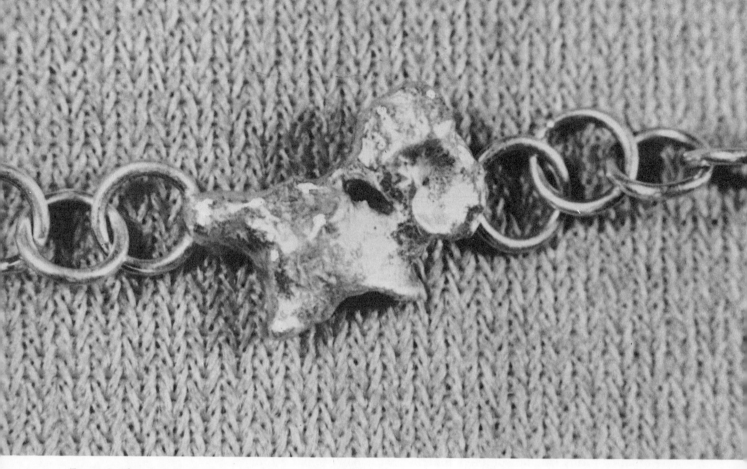

Figure 9. This chain has jump rings soldered to large chunks of silver produced by fusion.

sprinkle them lightly with the same flux you used in casting; heat them until the metal just begins to melt, and then pull the torch away quickly. The trick is to use the torch in such a way that the pieces melt only enough to hold them together without losing too much detail of the castings or winding up as one large lump of metal. The large chunks of silver in the chain shown in Figure 9 were produced by fusion.

5. Two different metal castings can be soldered together (gold and silver, silver and bronze) with silver solder in the sweat-soldering or appliqué technique to provide yet another distinguished form for jewelry.

After soldering on whatever findings, if any, are needed (joint, catch and pin for a brooch; a loop for a pendant; backs for cuff links; ear wire or clips for earrings; etc.) there should be little more to do than to file and sand rough spots, pickle the article, then buff, polish and, if desired, antique it.

Chapter Two

CUTTLEFISH BONE CASTING

WHAT IT IS

The cuttlefish is a squidlike sea mollusk with an internal shell that is often used as an easily learned and inexpensive means for casting jewelry. One side of the shell is thin but hard; the other side is relatively thick and softer with a texture very much like styrofoam. The bone has the ability of withstanding great heat, and the softer side retains any impression made in it. Thus, for example, if it is dented with a fingernail, it keeps the indentation and does not return to its original contour. This feature, as you will see, makes it useful for casting jewelry.

In addition to its simplicity and low cost, the advantage of cuttlefish bone casting is that it affords the beginner a chance to practice designing models of jewelry to be cast. Although not employed in drop casting discussed in Chapter 1 and another form of which will be discussed in Chapter 4, the designing of models is definitely the first step in this and every other form of casting in this book. One disadvantage of cuttlefish bone casting is that only relatively simple and small models may be cast by this method. This does not, however, exclude the possibility of making a large piece of jewelry from a large model. To do this, the procedure is to carefully cut the model into parts—each one of which fits into a pair of bones. Wax models can be cut with a sharp, thin knife; wood, plastic or metal models, with a

*Figure 10.
Small, medium
and large
cuttlefish bones.*

fine jeweler's saw blade. After the parts are cast, they are soldered together to form the large piece of jewelry. All indications of the soldering can then be filed, sanded and polished away. This approach will work only with gold, silver and pewter, for each of these metals has a color-matching solder which brass and bronze do not.

Everything cast by the bone process must be kept fairly simple because the bones are incapable of picking up complex details (*e.g.,* intricate surface textures) from a model. In addition, the bone-casting process depends entirely on gravity to pull the molten metal down into the mold or impression made by the model. It therefore cannot be expected that the molten metal will flow upward to fill any cavities above the main bulk of the mold, nor will it fill any thin, sharp curves that twist or coil in on themselves. Another disadvantage may be that a pair of bones can be used only once to produce one casting since great wear and tear occurs on the soft tissue through and into which the molten metal flows. Thus, in casting a matching pair of earrings, cuff links or similar parts for another jewelry item, two pairs of bones must be used. Models made of sturdy material can, of course, be used over and over again.

WHAT IS REQUIRED

1. You will need metal for casting and the same melting dish, crucible, charcoal block and tongs you previously used for drop casting. If the charcoal block is to be used again, be sure that the depression in the block is large enough to hold a fairly substantial amount of metal. There must be sufficient molten metal not only to fill the mold but also the gateway (hereafter referred to as the "gate") through which the metal flows from the charcoal block down to the mold. The weight of this metal in the gate helps

gravity fill the mold. This need to have sufficient metal for the gate also applies if you are using a melting dish or crucible in which to melt the metal.

2. Cuttlefish bones, sold by the piece or the pound, are available in three basic sizes which have reference to the length of the bones (see Figure 10). As a general rule, the longer they are the wider they are, as follows: small (5 to 6 inches), medium (6 to 7 inches), large (7 to 8 or 9 inches). The medium and large sizes are recommended. While two bones are needed for a single casting, it is often possible to cut a large bone in half at its greatest width and use the two halves for a relatively small casting.

3. A sheet of fine sandpaper and a smooth, flat, wood board large enough so that the sandpaper can be tacked onto it and will lie perfectly flat.

4. A few wooden match sticks or round wooden toothpicks for a purpose that will be explained shortly.

5. During the casting procedure, the bones must be firmly supported in an upright position so that the molten metal can be poured into the gate without causing the bones to topple over. The way to accomplish this is to place clean earth, clean sand, plaster of Paris, coarse salt or any other suitable material in a container of any shape that need be only long, wide and deep enough that the supporting material can be packed tightly around the bones to hold them securely in position.

6. Iron binding wire (18 to 22 gauge) with which to tie the bones together.

7. Material from which to construct the model. Of course, a piece of simple jewelry that you already have—such as a plain wedding band, a signet ring, a ring without a gemstone or any other jewelry article without complex structural details or without findings attached—can serve as a model for bone casting. Other than that, this method of casting depends on models carved from hard substances. If you have the required tools, these substances may be hardwood; lucite or plexiglas; sculpstone or similar materials sold under various trade names; chunks of such soft metals as lead, white metal and what is called "technique" metal; or hard carving wax. Of all these materials, the author strongly recommends hard carving wax primarily because most beginners generally want to go on to the lost-wax casting procedure which, as its name implies, mainly involves wax, and, that being the case, the novice might just as well start learning from the very beginning how to use the tools and how to carve the wax.

Inasmuch as carving wax has been recommended, a special word should be said about it. Carving wax comes in the form of blocks and bars (see Figure 11). It is also available in other shapes and sizes and in three grades of hardness, as will be explained in the next chapter. For bone casting, the hardest grade in block form is recommended since small chunks can be cut from it for rings and other small jewelry and large slices can be cut from it to make good-sized brooches, pendants and similar pieces.

8. A hacksaw is very useful for cutting chunks or slices from the hard wax block. The saw will, of course cut only in a straight line. For the rough shaping of the curved outline of a wax model from a chunk or slice of wax, a thin spiral-tooth saw blade or a No. 4 jeweler's saw blade—either of which will fit into a jeweler's saw frame—works well because the wax does not clog the teeth as easily as it does blades with fine teeth.

Figure 11.
Block and bar of
carving wax.
Note that chunks
have been
cut from the block.

9. A half-round wax file or even a shoemaker's file (see Figure 12) is useful in the early shaping stages for establishing flat surfaces or rounding contours. The teeth of these files do not so readily fill with wax, and if they do, they can be cleaned with a file brush (usually called a "file card"). Of the two files, the wax file, with its slimmer, tapered body, is more useful than the shoemaker's file.

10. There are a variety of wax carving tools and knives available. (These are discussed and illustrated in Chapter Four.) However, a pocket knife or other knife with a thin, sharp blade or the knife set (see Figure 13) sold in hobby shops and by suppliers of casting tools and materials will serve the purpose in carving the simple models to which bone casting is restricted.

11. Sandpaper or sanding cloth (preferable because it is more flexible) works well in removing the marks left by a knife or file. A small piece wrapped around a flat chunk of metal or wood will do much to refine flat

Figure 12. Half-round wax file (left) and
shoemaker's file are useful.

Figure 13. X-Acto knife and blade
set is handy.

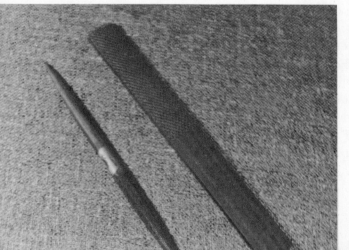

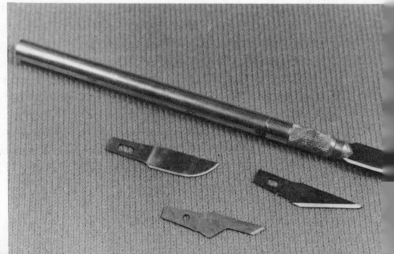

surfaces as well as to round the edges and outside corners or to round any outside (convex) curve. When wrapped around short lengths of wood dowels or metal rods of different diameters, they are very helpful in refining the contours of inside (concave) curves.

12. Powdered graphite is often used for reasons explained in the "how-to" section of this chapter. The powdered graphite used to lubricate door locks and sold in a squeezable plastic tube in most hardware and automobile supply stores is perfectly adequate.

13. A small tube of Chinese white watercolor paint or a small jar of white tempera paint might be worth having, again for reasons given in the "how-to" section which follows.

THE HOW-TO OF CUTTLEFISH BONE CASTING

The first step is to make a model. Since hard carving wax was recommended, a model made from that material will be discussed and demonstrated. And since cuttlefish bones lend themselves admirably to the casting of finger rings, we will carve a ring. You, of course, need not duplicate the model shown. In fact (and which cannot be emphasized too much), it is hoped you will feel adventurous enough to create your own design, keeping in mind the limitations of bone casting as set forth in the opening section of this chapter. It is suggested that you start with a drawing, however rough, of what you intend to make. This can be done right on the wax block by placing a dab of white watercolor paint on the block and smearing it around with a finger. While the paint is still wet, use a pencil to roughly outline the top view of the model you have in mind. You may have to go over the lines a few times because the paint is wet, but if you wait until it dries it becomes brittle and chips off easily. Figure 14 shows the outlines of two models which provide an indication of how large a chunk of wax must be cut to make the model. Always leave some excess wax around the entire outline of the model so that there is enough to carve away before getting down to the exact size the model should be. Once the chunk is cut, a side view of the model can be drawn on one side of it, and any excess wax can be cut off for future use if it is large enough. The paint will wash away with water, but an outline from the pencil will remain on the wax as a guide for your initial carving.

It is worthwhile digressing for a moment to point out that hard carving wax is not brittle, does not easily chip or crack and, with reasonable handling, can withstand all the tooling operations applied to hard wood. Thus, in addition to sawing, whittle-type carving, filing, sanding and the like, it can also be drilled with hand and power tools and turned to the desired diameter on a wood lathe, using normal woodworking tools.

Once the chunk of wax has been cut from the block, you are ready to begin work on the ring model. The first step is cut out the hole for the finger. This can be done with a sharp carving knife or with a wood bit chucked in a hand drill or brace or in a drill press driven at slow speed. It is difficult to tell you exactly how large this hole should be except to first indicate that the knuckle of every finger of most people's hands, except the pinkie, is larger than the fleshy part where a ring is usually worn. Second,

Figure 14.
Drawing on wax block
with white
watercolor paint.

when metal is cast by any casting method it shrinks by as much as 1 per cent from the over-all size of its wax model. Hence, if the center hole of a model ring is initially made large enough to slip comfortably over the knuckle of a finger (again with the exception of the pinkie, where it should be smaller than the fleshy part) it will, when cast, be so large as to constantly twist around on the finger. And, finally, it is always easier to enlarge the finger hole of a metal ring than it is to make it smaller, providing its shank is not initially made too thin. The best procedure, therefore, is to make the finger hole just shy of fitting over the knuckle of the ring finger and not to carve any part of the ring shank too thin.

Now the job is to shape the wax model to the ring model you have in mind. The corners of the chunk can be sawed off. All curves and curvatures can be formed with coarse files, with the knife or with any other usable tools that are on hand or can be improvised. The improvisations that can be devised are virtually unlimited. If you permit imagination plus some experimentation to be your guide, you may be surprised at what you can come up with. As you move ahead, fine sandpaper can materially aid in refining the model. So can the carving knife used in a light scraping rather than cutting action. Pieces of cheesecloth tacked onto a piece of flat wood, wound around short lengths of wood dowels of different diameters or even around a finger work exceedingly well in removing the marks left by the files, sanding materials or knife. Then gently rub the wax with a small piece of smooth, finely woven cloth (silk preferably) or a piece of wet absorbent cotton to still further smooth and refine the wax surfaces. Figure 15 shows the finished wax model of the ring.

Next, the cuttlefish bones in which the ring will be cast must be selected. It is important to remember that the soft, domed surface of each bone will be sanded flat, and that the model will be pressed down into each of them for half of its height. Therefore the bones selected must be thick enough in their midsection to allow for this. Once you have selected the bones, which should be as equal in size as possible, saw off their ends with a hacksaw or any fine-toothed metal cutting blade. Go slow when sawing through the hard surface of the bones because this is very brittle and may split or break away to such an extent as to make the bone useless. With the sheet of fine sandpaper tacked to a piece of wood as recom-

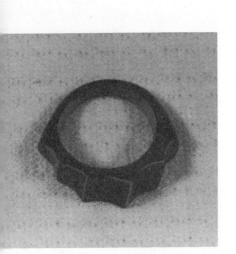

Figure 15.
Finished wax model
of the ring
being used for
demonstration.

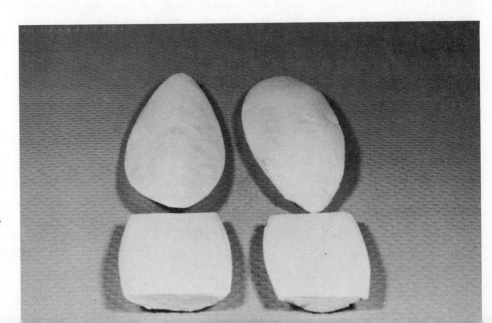

Figure 16.
Cuttlefish bones
cut down
and sanded flat.

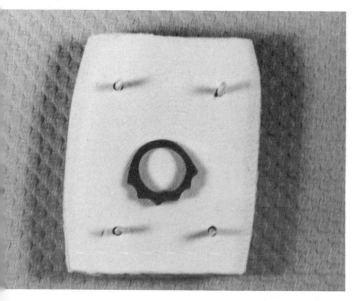

Figure 17. Wax pattern and keys.

Figure 18. Bones pressed together with X's and marks for the gate.

mended earlier, sand the soft surface of each bone absolutely flat, using a rotary motion. (See Figure 16.)

You are now ready to position the ring model in one of the bones. In this casting process, the rule is that the thickest or heaviest part of any model should always be placed so that it will be in the lower part of the bones when they are stood upright later. This does not apply, of course, to a model such as a wedding ring, which has the same height and thickness all around its circumference.

Place the model in one bone so that it is equidistant from the sides of the bone. There should be a space of ¾ in. to 1 in. between the heaviest, or lower, part of the model and the lower end of the bone. There should also be at least 1½ inches between the top end of the model and the top end of the bone where the gate for the molten metal will be formed. With the model properly positioned, proceed to press it down with your fingers until half its body around its entire perimeter is set firmly in the bone. Next cut four wooden matchsticks or round toothpicks about ⅝ in. long, sharpen their ends and press them into the bone holding the wax model as shown in Figure 17. With a pencil mark the top end of each bone with an X.

Continue by placing the two bones together—gingerly at first—so that their outer edges are in good alignment. Then place both bones in the palm of one hand, interlock the fingers of both hands and, exerting pressure with the palms of *both* hands, press the two bones together as tightly as you can. Sitting and placing your clasped hands between your knees, which you use to exert more pressure, will help in getting the kind of mold that will result in producing a more perfect casting. If you find that the wooden pegs are too long to get the bones firmly together, cut them shorter so that they do not interfere with the prescribed procedure. When you feel you have made the best possible mold impression, mark off with a pencil the place where the gate will be cut (see Figure 18). The width of this upper

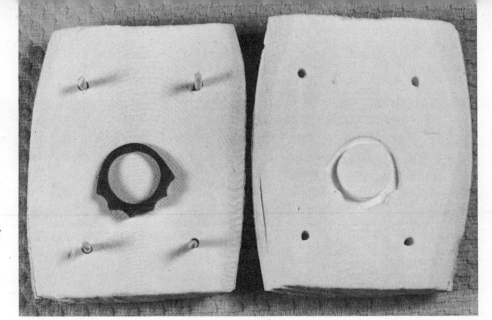

Figure 19.
Bones apart after
being
pressed together.

end of the gate should be about ⅝ in. Now carefully pull the two bones apart so as not to change the outline of the mold. They should look as shown in Figure 19.

Dusting the mold with powdered graphite helps in producing a mold with smoother surfaces. Do this after gently lifting the wax model out of the bone. Do not use too much graphite as this could change the shape of the mold. Blow away any excess or else carefully brush it away with a soft camel's-hair, artist-type brush. Gently place the wax model back into the first bone in exactly the same position as it was the first time, and press the two bones together again so as to fix the graphite into the bone tissue. Then separate the bones and remove the wax model as before.

Cutting the gate and vents in the bones, as illustrated in Figure 20, follows. Perform these operations with a sharp knife. The funnel-shaped gate should be cut down and into the top of the ring mold in each bone. First outline the gate with a pencil or the point of your knife blade. Then carve out the gate with the knife. Note that the gate becomes shallower as it reaches the mold and narrows down to about 1/8 to 3/16 in. at the top of the mold. Vents are cut into both bones as shown in the same photograph to provide escape paths for air and gases that might otherwise be trapped in the mold and produce an incomplete casting. Be sure that the gate and mold are perfectly clear of all bits and pieces of bone cuttings—blow them

Figure 20. Gate and vents cut (top) and
bones tied together (bottom).

Figure 21. Tied bones standing in sand,
ready for the casting process.

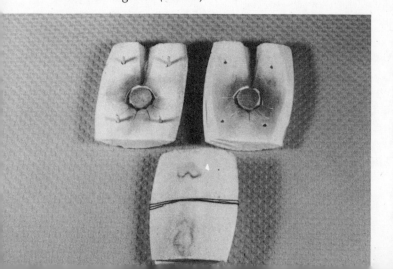

Figure 22.
Bones untied after
casting.

out or carefully pick them out with the knife point or a sharp-pointed tweezer. With the wax model removed, and using the pegs as guides, place the bones together and tie them tightly in this position with binding wire as also shown in Figure 20 (bottom). Place them, with the gate up, in the utensil along with the material you are using to support the bones for the casting process (see Figure 21).

In bone casting, the simplest way to determine the amount of metal needed for the casting is to use your eyes. Cut pieces or use scraps of metal that you feel will be a little more than enough to produce the ring or any other model (sterling silver was used for the demonstration ring). Then add an amount of metal that, in your judgment, will almost fill the gate. It is always better to melt more metal rather than less in order to ensure a complete casting, bearing in mind that whatever you do not pour or later cut away from the casting can be cleaned and cast again. If the metal you are casting is not clean, pickle it, wash it in clean water and place it in your melting dish or crucible. The melting of the metal, including its dusting with flux and its pouring, is the same as was prescribed for drop casting, except that in this case the molten metal is poured into the gate formed in the two bones.

Wait until the bones have cooled enough to be handled comfortably before untieing them to see what you achieved. When separated, they will appear very much as they do in Figure 22. Wash the casting with detergent and a bristle brush, pickle it and then wash it again. The metal formed in the gate is called a "sprue." Cut it and any other projections off with a jeweler's saw. Use files, sanding cloths, buffing and polishing compounds and equipment to refine the casting as you would a piece of constructed jewelry. If you wish—and depending on the type of ring you have cast—

Figure 23. Demonstration ring is finished.

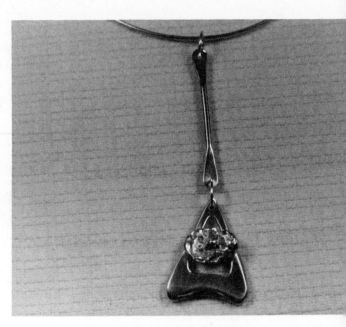

Figure 24. Pendant necklace made with pewter.

you can now add other details, including a gemstone. The finished demonstration ring is shown in Figure 23.

In the pendant of Figure 24 the triangular portion—without the decorative attachment—was carved from wax and cast with pewter in cuttlefish bones. The decorative attachment is pewter that was drop-cast in cold water and then soldered with pewter flux and solder to the triangular portion. The rest of the pendant consists of jump rings and wire constructed from pewter wire. The ends of the heavier round wire were flattened with a ball peen hammer. The holes for the jump rings were drilled with a No. 57 twist drill. The purpose in demonstrating this pendant is to indicate the added flexibility you can gain when you combine several jewelry-making and casting processes and add a bit of imagination. Another example are the pendants and earrings shown in Figure 25 in which gemstones are set in drop-cast silver. This was a student's first experience with this process.

Figure 25.
Pendants and earrings of
drop-cast silver.

Chapter Three

INTRODUCTION TO THE LOST WAX PROCESS

WHAT IT IS

From this point on, the book will deal with both the creative and mechanical procedures involved in the lost wax process of casting. The process is actually centuries old and was practiced—as it still is—on every continent in the world. Today, it remains the principal method by which not only jewelry is cast but by which metal sculpture of every description and dimension is also cast. In a subsequent chapter, some of the different types of equipment employed in the casting of jewelry and small sculpture will be discussed. However, regardless of the kind of equipment used, there are seven basic steps that are followed in producing jewelry or sculpture by this technique. Each step will later be described in detail; for now let us just define each one briefly:

STEP 1. Creating the wax model. There are two major methods: the carving, or "cutting away," method introduced in cuttlefish bone casting, but which, in the lost wax process, allows the craftsman much greater freedom in design; and the "building up" method to which you will be introduced shortly.

STEP 2. Spruing the model. This is the procedure of attaching wax to the model to form one or more gates to the mold so that molten metal can easily enter the mold.

STEP 3. Venting the model. In this step, thin wax wires are attached to the wax model, when and where needed, to provide escapeways for the air and gases in the mold so that they do not block the molten metal from entering and filling the mold.

STEP 4. Determining the amount of metal needed to complete the entire casting. There are two main ways of doing this and both will be discussed.

STEP 5. Investing the wax model. This is the act of encasing the model, sprue(s), and vents (if any) in a creamy mixture of a heat-resisting, plasterlike material called "investment."

STEP 6. Burnout. In this step, all the wax encased in the investment (as well as any wax residues) is burned out to make room for the molten metal, which is why this mode of casting is called the "lost wax process."

STEP 7. Casting. In this operation, the spaces previously occupied in the investment by wax are now filled with metal through the use of some kind of force or pressure-producing equipment.

THE WAXES USED

There are so many different waxes of different colors, in different shapes, of different degrees of hardness, softness and flexibility—along with other characteristics—that listing and explaining them all would not only result in producing a catalog equivalent in part to those published by the suppliers of casting materials but would also almost fill the remaining pages of this book. The most practical approach, in the author's opinion, is to indicate those that he has found to be most useful and workable in his casting experience, and to cite those he believes the student of casting should avoid and why. This is not intended by any means to discourage the student from engaging in his own experimentation and deciding on his own preferences.

So far as the colors of commercially supplied waxes are concerned, these vary from manufacturer to manufacturer even though the basic characteristics of the wax are the same or similar. Thus, in the last chapter,

Figure 26.
Hard carving wax
in the form
of ring tubes.

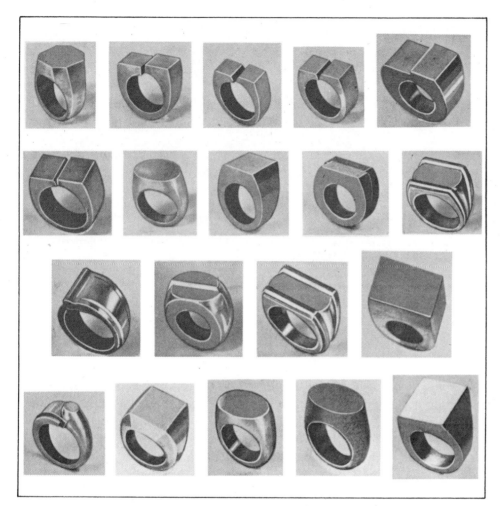

Figure 27.
Hard carving wax
in the form
of roughly shaped rings.

for example, hard carving wax was recommended for bone casting. The hardest is available in at least three colors: green, brown and red. Less hard carving wax is supplied in purple or another color, and the least hard is made in blue or still another color. For carving jewelry or small sculpture models, the author's choice is the hardest grade wax available regardless of color. Just be sure it is *carving* wax, for not all wax that is hard and inflexible can be carved. If it is not, it may be so brittle that it chips and cracks when you try to cut it.

In addition to the block and bar shapes that hard carving wax comes in, it is also sold in the form of ring tubes from which pieces can be cut to be carved primarily into rings (see Figure 26). It is also offered as roughly preshaped rings, called "master rings," which include wedding bands, rings for gemstones, signet rings and the like (see Figure 27). Since in working with the ring tubes and master rings you do save some carving time, and because you still must provide the artistry and skill to model them into attractive jewelry articles, the author has no objection to them. He has, in fact, cast a few rings that started out as preshaped master rings. Bear in mind, however, that you pay extra for these special shapes and that they limit you pretty much to the making of rings. And, finally, offered for sale

Figure 28.
Wax sheets come in
assorted gauges.

are *completely* finished hard wax models of rings, pins, pendants and other jewelry objects which the author would discourage anyone from using because they totally eliminate the personal creativity of the craftsman and leave him or her with little more to do than to proceed with Steps 2 through 7 above which are mainly mechanical in nature.

Carving, or cutting away bits of wax with knives, files and other tools, is only one basic method of model making. The other, and actually opposite technique, is the building up of a model by adding wax to wax until you have a model you wish to cast. Here again a large variety of waxes in different colors, shapes, sizes, degrees of hardness plus other characteristics, are available, and here again the author will conserve space and time by indicating those he believes will work well for the student caster because they worked well for him from the time he was a novice.

One form of build-up wax is supplied in square or rectangular sheets of different gauges (thicknesses). It is sold in boxes containing sheets of all one gauge or of assorted gauges. The recommended initial purchase is a box

Figure 29. Wax wires come in round,
half-round, square, and rectangular form.

Figure 30. Utility wax and sprue wax
are useful in model making.

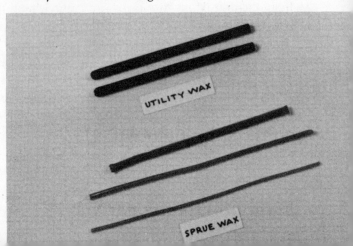

Figure 31.
Homemade wax mixture
in casserole.

of either the square or rectangular pink wax sheets in assorted gauges (see Figure 28). There are wax wires (from 4 to about 5 inches long) offered in different gauges and in these forms: round, half-round, square and rectangular (see Figure 29). It is well to have an assortment of round, half-round and square wire on hand. The rectangular wire (which the photograph shows) was cut with a scissors from wax sheets. Another useful kind of build-up wax to have is either inlay casting wax or utility wax in stick or rod form, plus what is called sprue wax in 8 and 10 gauge (see Figure 30). A small supply of sticky wax in sheet or rod form is very handy for joining waxes together. The precise uses of all the build-up waxes will be explained later.

There is a relatively inexpensive wax that the author and some other casters use in ways to be explained later that can easily be prepared by the beginner. Equal parts of paraffin (sold in many supermarkets and in shops that sell candle-making supplies) and beeswax (available from jewelry supply houses) are melted in a double boiler and are mixed together by stirring them well with a table knife, a slat of wood or any suitable implement. The mixture is then poured into a porcelain casserole or a small enameled cooking pot, preferably one with a spout, where it is allowed to cool and harden (see Figure 31). This wax is a fairly good substitute for the inlay casting or utility waxes. Any wax remaining in the double boiler or on the stirring utensil can be removed with hot water.

Having the waxes recommended above, as a starting inventory, will equip you to design three or four dozen different and handsome jewelry models, and perhaps many more.

Chapter Four

MODEL MAKING FOR THE LOST WAX PROCESS

THE CARVING METHOD

You have already met this method in the chapter on cuttlefish bone casting. You were cautioned, however, to keep your design simple because cuttlefish bones can pick up only the simplest details from a model. And since that casting process depends upon gravity to pull the molten metal into the mold, you cannot expect the molten metal to flow upward to completely fill the mold. There are no such restrictions on models created for the lost wax casting process. Models may be carved or built up in any way that will produce results pleasing to the craftsman's eye or artistic taste. They may have openings of any size or shape, bends and curves of every description and any kind of textured surface or other intricacy that the craftsman can produce. The fact is that the lost wax process of casting is so capable of reproducing even the minutest detail that if the craftsman leaves fingerprints on a wax model, they will without a doubt appear on his metal casting. For this reason—and regardless of what model-making method is used—it is wise to establish the practice of removing all defects from the wax model before casting it into metal, because it is then much more difficult to eliminate dents, scratches and other imperfections.

In addition to the knife and files mentioned in Chapter 2, there are other tools that are very useful in carving the more complex kinds of mod-

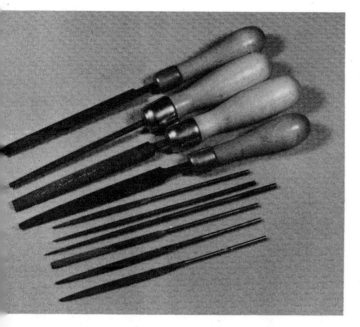

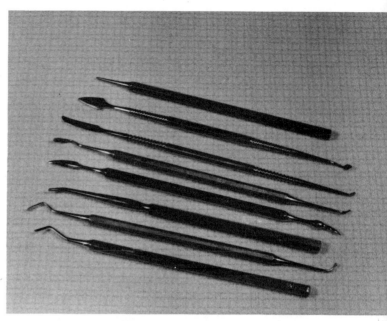

Figure 32. *Small files of different shapes are handy for cutting away wax.*

Figure 33. *Many carving tools are borrowed from dental profession.*

els. The purpose in illustrating or suggesting these tools is not to send you rushing out to buy them (unless, of course, you wish to do so), but rather to give you some idea of what you want to look for, what you may find around your home and/or what you may be able in some way to adapt or improvise. By no means do you need all these tools immediately, if ever. The photographs show items the author has accumulated—often one or two at a time—over a number of years. There are, for example, different-shaped small files, including needle files, that are quite helpful for cutting away wax in tighter places than the shoemaker's or wax files can reach (see Figure 32). The author bought the least expensive files with the coarsest teeth he could find. Although their teeth fill up with wax rather rapidly, it is no problem to clean them out with a file card or with the type of wire brush used to brush up suede shoes or other suede articles.

Then there are the tools that are basically designed to aid in imparting fine, detailed carvings and surface textures to jewelry models, although a few are also used in the wax build-up process. These are sold by casting supply companies as well as by dental supply companies inasmuch as most, if not all, are tools used by dentists and dental mechanics in the fabrication of gold inlay fillings, caps for teeth and dental bridges. It was actually the dental profession that contributed much of the modern casting materials and equipment that have been adopted and adapted by today's commercial jewelry producers and individual jewelry casters (see Figure 33). Perhaps you may be able to persuade your dentist to let you have the wax tools that are no longer of any use to him. You might also look around your home to see if there may be certain items that can be adapted, or serve as they are, as substitutes for some of those in the illustration.

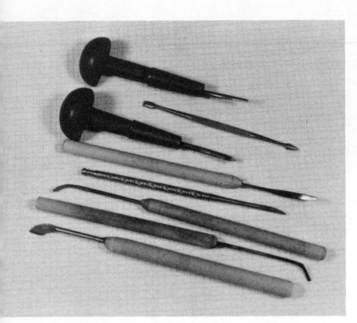

Figure 34. Carving tools can be improvised from many sources.

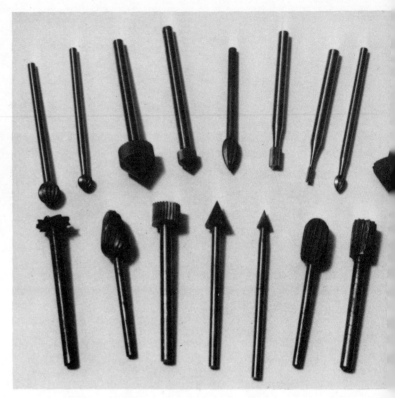

Figure 35. Jeweler's burrs and rotary files are used with flexible shaft.

Figure 34 shows carving tools that the author improvised from tools in an old manicure set, from old nutpicks and from other items whose origin he cannot now recall. They were either kept as they were or reshaped with the help of a bench grinder, carborundum sharpening stones and sanding cloth. In some cases handles had to be provided by drilling a hole of suitable diameter and length in one end of a short wood dowel and permanently fixing one end of the improvised tool in the dowel with epoxy cement. In the same photograph are two old metal engraving tools (burins) that the author bought at a local thrift shop. They have proved excellent for cutting thin lines into wax. You may be able to fashion your engraving tools from some metal or metal objects you have lying around in your basement or attic.

If you are fortunate enough to have a flexible shaft outfit of some kind, there are jeweler's burrs and rotary files with coarse cuts that come in a large variety of shapes and sizes, produced to be used as accessories with a flexible shaft for wax carving (see Figure 35). They are extremely useful for the rapid removal of wax, for texturing wax surfaces, and for related operations. Finally, there are rather inexpensive cutters used in preparing linoleum blocks for block printing, as there also are small chip-carving tools for wood carving that can also serve as practical wax-carving implements.

Before going on to the build-up technique, it would be worth your while to pause at this point and do some practice and experimenting with

Figure 36. Four jewelry models carved from hard wax.

the carving method: first, because you will learn more about this method and the variety of design possibilities it offers; second, because you should be thoroughly familiar with the tools you have and what they can do for you in putting your ideas down in wax; and third, because much of what you learn from this practice and experimentation will be applicable to the building up of wax models in which carving is often employed as a planned part of the models or to enhance their appearance. In addition, the models you carve can serve two other useful purposes: (1) those that please you can be set aside for casting into metal when you get to that procedure; (2) those that you would rather not cast can be used for practice in spruing a model, which is Step 2 in the lost wax process.

Figure 36 shows jewelry models carved from hard wax. They are simple, quite unassuming and presented solely to indicate a few of the different pieces of jewelry that can be carved and some of the treatments that can be given them, with the hope that this will stimulate your own ingenuity. The model on the left is that of a pin or brooch. Note that holes or negative areas have intentionally been made in the pattern to contrast with the positive areas and thus lend visual interest. After it is cast, small stones or pearls can, if desired, be set in several places to enhance the article still more. The top center model is one that can serve several purposes. A few possibilities are: It could be the central, decorative ornament soldered onto a bracelet fabricated from plain sheet metal; with the addition of a link or links, it could be one of a number of similarly shaped and carved parts for a link bracelet or necklace; or it could be used simply as a charm dangling from a charm bracelet. Two such models that are the same in all respects except that they face in opposite directions when placed side by side could be used to make earrings or cuff links. The pendant model on the right was constructed to show that the hole for the jump ring from which the pendant would suspend from a chain can be made right in the wax prior to casting. The small facets made by a tool in the various sections will be places from which light will be reflected in many directions when the metal casting is completed. The remaining model is obviously that of a ring.

All the patterns, except the ring, originated from a sheet of wax, 3/16-in. thick, cut with a hacksaw from the broad, flat face of a wax block held in a vise. Pieces were then cut from this sheet somewhat larger than the intended patterns. The ring started out as a chunk of wax, 1⅛ in. x 1⅛ in. x ½ in., cut from the same block. After all the carving was done on the face of the top three models in the photograph, the back of each was slimmed down and hollowed out as much as was practical without making it too thin or spoiling the face of the model by cutting through to it. Incidentally, a good way to tell if you are cutting too deeply—whether from the front *or* the back of the model—is to hold the wax up to a source of light. Obviously, the more light you can see shining through any part of it, the thinner the wax is at that place—which is a warning that perhaps you had better stop where you are.

It is quite possible that some models, or parts thereof, should not be thinned or slimmed down because, in so doing, the planned jewelry design may be adversely affected. On the other hand, there are reasons for reducing the bulk of a model that deserve consideration: One is the amount of metal required to cast a model which, in terms of gold and silver, can be an important economic factor based on the cost of these metals. Another is that since all jewelry is meant to be worn by a person, the bulk and weight of a piece of jewelry (*e.g.*, earrings, cuff links, a ring, a pendant) should not be such that it cannot be worn in complete comfort. There is also a factor in designing jewelry to be cast that was mentioned earlier which is significant enough to be mentioned again: the over-all dimensions of a model—that is, its size in terms of its length, width, diameter, circumference, etc.—should not exceed the capacity of the equipment in which it is to be cast unless you are willing to cut the model apart and cast the sections separately with the idea of soldering them together in order to produce the complete jewelry article.

Apart from these few guidelines, it is not possible to provide an exact step-by-step account of how to achieve precisely the same wax models as those shown. Remember, we are involved in creating one-of-a-kind jewelry. Try as you might, you could not possibly duplicate every single detail that one craftsman puts in his model any more than he could duplicate those in yours. There is a way for this to be done that is primarily used commercially, but the procedures and the equipment utilized are outside the scope of this book. That is why, as was stressed earlier, it is so important for you to practice and experiment with what tools you have, for that is the only way to learn what the tools can do and what you can accomplish with them.

THE BUILDING-UP METHOD

The principal aspects of wax build-up that differentiate it from the other method are that it involves waxes initially much softer than the carving waxes and, being softer, much more flexible—some sheets and wires will bend at room temperature (70 to 72 degrees) or from the warmth of your hands. Higher heat in another form is used to soften the waxes still further for greater flexibility . . . to join separate pieces of wax together . . . to add details such as textures, beads of wax, built-up contours and configurations . . . or to melt the wax away from a surface even to such an extent that a hole is deliberately made as part of a design.

Because they are relatively soft, build-up waxes should be worked on a perfectly smooth surface that can easily be kept clean. Smoothness is important because the sheets, wires and other wax forms you are modeling with may pick up textures, dents and nicks that you may not want in your casting. Cleanliness is important not only for the surface on which you are modeling but to the area around it, since these waxes can easily pick up bits of dirt, metal and other debris that may have gone unnoticed and end up in the metal casting to spoil the appearance of an otherwise well-made piece of jewelry.

Assuming that you are building up a model that is essentially to be flat over all (*e.g.*, a brooch, pendant, parts of a bracelet, necklace, etc.), there are materials that will work well such as a square of plain ceramic tile, a piece of sheet plastic or a piece of the material used to surface kitchen counters, plus many others. The author's preference is for a piece of plate glass with beveled edges which can be bought in a store that sells glass and mirrors (window glass is fragile and breaks too easily). An extra advantage of plate glass is that if you sketch a jewelry design on paper, it can be placed under the glass (as shown in Figure 37) and the wax can be built

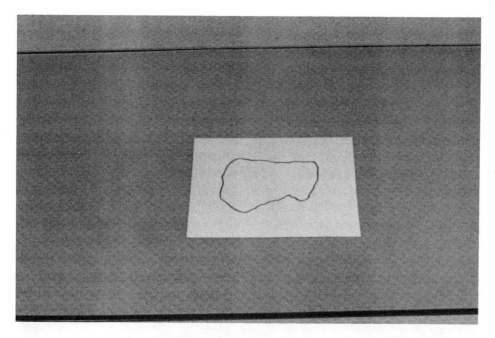

Figure 37.
Jewelry design is sketched
on paper and
placed under plate glass
as guide.

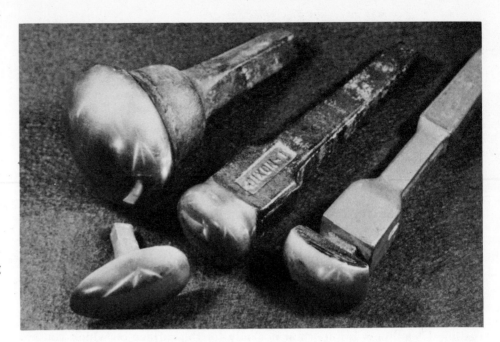

Figure 38.
Convex silversmithing
stakes.

up on the glass directly over the sketch, which thus acts as a guide in the
initial modeling stages, at least.

Let us assume, however, that you wish to build up a model that has—
from its front view—a convex contour (again a brooch, pendant, etc., as
before). You will need some object with a convex curved surface since it is
impractical to try to design this kind of form on a flat surface. As always,
there are items you can buy, that you already have or that you can improvise. Figure 38 shows several silversmithing stakes with different convex
surfaces as sold by many jewelry supply houses. On the other hand, much
less costly but equally serviceable substitutes are illustrated in Figure 39
below. On the left is part of a door knob mounted with screws onto a block
of wood; in the center is an implement that was retrieved from a cast-off
pan in which eggs were poached. The implement—the cup into which the
raw egg was dropped—had a small handle which was cut away. The cup
was filled with plaster of Paris into which one end of a dowel was placed
before the plaster hardened, with its other end glued with epoxy cement
into a wood block. On the right is a cork with a metal capping that came

Figure 39.
Improvised convex
surfaces as described
in text.

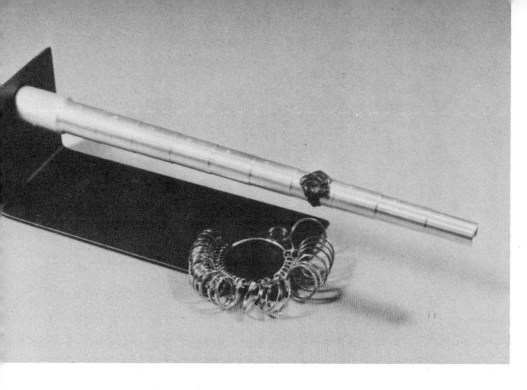

Figure 40.
Stepped ring mandrel
with ring and
ring sizer.

from a discarded water pitcher or some sort of utensil. The cork is also glued to a wood block. In front is a workshop-type shade for an electric bulb, also filled with plaster of Paris to add some weight and stability. Necessity plus a dash of thriftiness can truly be the mother of invention in many instances.

Suppose now that you wanted to build up a ring—again an operation that is extremely difficult unless you have an appropriate device on which to fashion it, and once again there are items you can buy. Figure 40 illustrates what is called a stepped ring mandrel specifically made for designing wax ring patterns. This untapered, base-mounted mandrel can be rotated on its mount so that you can work from above on the full circumference of the ring model; or it can be removed from its mount to be hand held. It is sized for rings (Sizes 4 through 13) that correspond to the sizes of a ring sizer (shown in the same photograph) employed in measuring fingers for rings. If you plan to make many rings, the mandrel and the ring sizer are both very useful implements to have. There is also the tapered ring mandrel (see Figure 41). While it is mainly used in constructing rings from

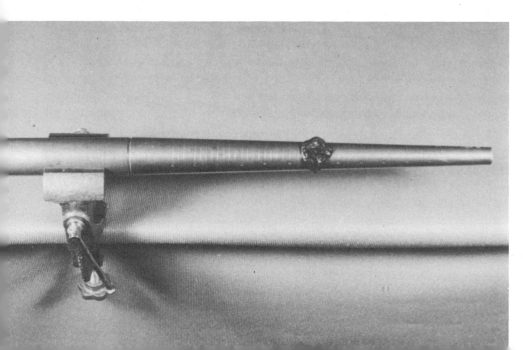

Figure 41.
Tapered ring mandrel
and wax ring.

 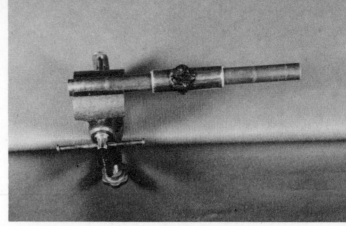

Figure 42. Carbon ring mandrel with wax ring.   *Figure 43. Improvised ring mandrel and wax ring.*

metal, there is no reason why rings cannot be built up on it from wax. It also is marked with ring sizes and can be hand held or fixed in a vise as shown. Then there is the base-mounted carbon mandrel used for soldering ring shanks and metal parts to the shank—again primarily in the jewelry construction process—that can also be utilized in building up a ring in wax (see Figure 42). It is not marked with graduated ring sizes, but note that a piece of household-type aluminum foil is placed between the wax ring model and the device to prevent the wax from sticking to the mandrel's carbon surface. To hold the foil tightly on the mandrel, use small pieces of cellophane tape at the ends of the foil where they will not interfere with the shaping of the ring's shank. By placing the required finger size of the ring sizer over (around) the carbon mandrel, a point can be marked on the foil where the ring should be modeled.

If you do not have, nor care to invest in, any of the above mandrels, there is a substitute that works quite well, although it does require a ring sizer so that you can measure both the intended ring finger and the mandrel to be improvised. The substitute consists of either a short length of wood dowel, metal rod or metal pipe about ½ inch in diameter, although only a ¼-in. diameter is required for a young child's ring. On this, carefully and tightly wrap 2-in.-wide, smooth-surfaced, gummed tape until you have almost reached the diameter of the ring size needed (see Figure 43). Use the ring sizer to make this determination after placing aluminum foil around the tape as explained with the carbon mandrel above. Which brings us to an important point that applies not only to this make-do mandrel but to all those mentioned: a ring wax model *should always be made one size smaller* than what a finger measures because the molten metal for the casting shrinks about that much when it cools. Thus, if a finger measures 7½, the ring model should be Size 7; if the finger measures 9, the ring model should be Size 8½. Obviously it will be necessary to alter the diameter of the tape on this improvised mandrel whenever you change from one size to another.

We will now describe some of the techniques, tools, equipment—as well as other pertinent matters—employed in the build-up process. The information developed is applicable, of course, to models of many different forms of jewelry. Since the first three demonstration items are to be essentially flat, a flat surface is used as the work surface. Whatever is used as the work surface—and this includes the convex surfaces and the ring mandrel employed—it is well that it be lightly lubricated with a fine oil or glycerin (pharmacies carry it) so that the wax does not stick. Commercial lubricants are also available from supply houses. The lubricant is applied with a clean cloth or piece of cotton, primarily to the section on which the model is to be worked up. Most of the lubricant should be wiped away so that only a thin film remains. The demonstration object starts out from a sheet of 18-ga. (ga. is the abbreviation for gauge) pink wax. A simple drawing has been made of the item's over-all outline and the first task is to cut the sheet to match this outline as closely as possible. Because sheet wax of 18 and thicker gauge is quite translucent, it is feasible to place the sheet over the drawing and lightly inscribe its outline on the wax with a scriber or any sharp-pointed tool. The sheet is then cut to the outline with a small scissors or a heated knife (see Figure 44). The how-to of heating the knife will be explained in a moment.

Now suppose a jewelry item is not to be entirely flat, but is to have some curvatures or contours to provide it with an individual character. Although somewhat soft and pliable, sheet wax (or wire) may not be soft or flexible enough to give the desired contours; so it must be further softened by a heat source. Note that this softening is temporary—the build-up waxes cool upon removal from the heat source and reharden to their original condition. One way to soften sheet wax or wire is to dip it into a container of warm water. This makes it pliable enough that you can contour it with your hands in almost any way you wish, including bending it over and/or around tools so as to obtain a particular form (e.g., a dome shape, ring shank, bracelet, etc.). Another way is to pass the sheet or wire back and forth quickly over or through the flame of an alcohol lamp or bunsen burner (see Figure 45). Care must be taken not to heat the wax to such an extent that it melts. A lighted candle, heat lamp or a 100-watt electric bulb will also work, but the recommendation is for an alcohol lamp or bunsen burner because each is useful for other operations as well as softening wax. For example, the knife mentioned above for cutting out an object's outline can be heated in the flame of the lamp or burner. Just heat the blade sufficiently to slice its way easily through the wax sheet. Too much heat will destroy

*Figure 44. Outline is cut from sheet wax
with scissors or heated knife.*   *Figure 45. Alcohol lamp and bunsen burner
have many uses in model making.*

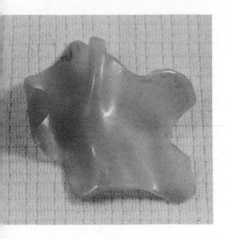

Figure 46.
Contoured wax sheet.

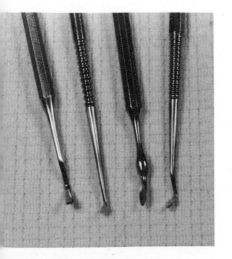

Figure 47.
Close-up view of
dental carving tools used
for texturing.

Figure 48.
Some homemade tools
similar to the
dental carving tools.

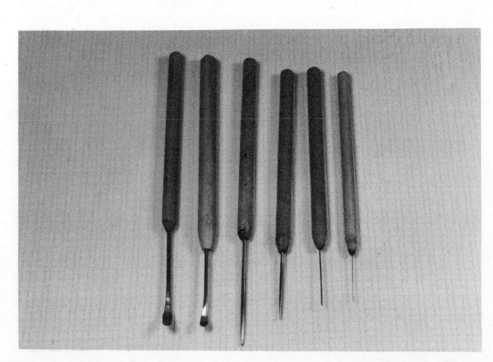

the blade's temper (stiffness). Figure 46 shows a model cut out of a sheet of 16-ga. wax and contoured by passing the wax over the flame of an alcohol lamp. (NOTE: *Should the wax sheet or wire become too soft to handle properly, reharden it by placing in cold water.*)

A design may call for an item of cast jewelry to have a texture on its front surface. The build-up process of wax-model-making is particularly good for producing textures as well as other details and features in wax models that cannot be done in any other way. Textures can be created in several ways. They can be *cut in* with one or more carving tools, they can be *melted in* with heated tools, or melted wax can be deposited on the wax surface to *build up* the textures. Figure 47 shows a close-up view of the ends of some of the dental carving tools previously shown in Figure 33. While they can carve the texture, they can also be heated so as to melt-in the texture as well as to carry melted wax to the model to build up the texture and other features. Figure 48 illustrates some homemade tools that can be used to obtain similar results. These are exclusive of the improvised wax carvers shown before in Figure 34. The upper two tools were hammered and filed out of 10-ga. and 12-ga. copper wire respectively, to form small spatulas and glued into dowels with epoxy cement. The four lower tools illustrated are different-sized sewing needles also cemented into dowels. These make-do implements are mainly useful when heated.

Based upon previous explanation, little should have to be said about how to carve a texture or other details into a wax surface with unheated carving tools. Using sheet wax at least 18-ga. or thicker, these unheated tools can be employed to carve little hills and valleys that run in one direction, in winding directions, or that crisscross each other in a variety of directions—or whatever other approach suggests itself to you. As for heated tools, other than a knife, the proper way to heat them is to hold them in a flame for a few seconds at least $\frac{1}{2}$ inch from their working ends or tips (see Figure 49). Practice will soon teach you how much to heat them in order that they will work as they should. Once they are heated, run them

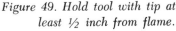
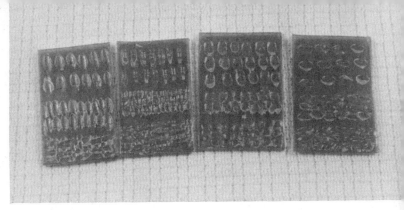

Figure 49. Hold tool with tip at least ½ inch from flame.

Figure 50. Samples of wax surfaces with tool meltings.

along the wax surface as you would the cold carving tools. The wax surface will melt and be thrust aside to form little hills and valleys. Reheat the tool as often as is necessary to produce the desired results. The tip of the heated tool may also be applied to the wax surface as you would a writing implement to a sheet of paper to produce a series of dots. The tool will melt craterlike indentations in the wax that can be closely spaced, touch one another, or overlap each other—each creating its own special texture (see Figure 50). In using a tool in this and some other techniques, you may find the tool becoming loaded with wax. To get rid of this wax, scrape it off with a knife or place the tool in hot water or in a flame and wipe the molten wax away with a cloth. It is always wise to keep your tools as clean as possible.

Textures and other features can also be built up by carrying molten wax to a model and "dribbling" or letting it trail off there. The applied wax, being hot, melts the wax it contacts and fuses with this wax to make a close bond between the two. One way of creating textures by this method is to heat the tool in the flame as before (a small spatula works best in this technique), apply the tool to a wax rod in order to pick up some wax, and briefly reheat the tool so as to keep the wax in a molten state. This wax is then trailed along the surface of the wax model. When you first try this, you may find that as you apply the hot wax it runs out on the surface in a kind of unshaped mass. As both the wax and tool cool, however, the wax can be textured by running the tool over the applied wax until it and the tool become too cold to work. Figure 51 shows a wax model that has been

*Figure 51.
Model has been textured
by running heated
tool over applied wax.*

Figure 52.
Wax melted in porcelain
casserole on
tripod with alcohol burner.

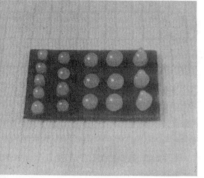

Figure 53.
These wax beads
were built up on the
small wax sheet.

Figure 54.
Wax ring
with built-up beads.

treated in this manner. One of the above steps can be eliminated by utilizing the homemade or any other suitable wax in the porcelain casserole or enameled pot referred to in Chapter 3. In this procedure, the wax container is placed on a tripod, and the wax is heated by an alcohol lamp or bunsen burner enough to get and keep it in a molten condition—*not* smoking or boiling (see Figure 52). The tool is heated as before, dipped into the melted wax to pick up some of it and then carried directly to the pattern without the need for reheating the tool. There it is dispersed as before.

Still another way to build up textures and other details on a wax model is to hold one end of a wax rod in a flame until some of it is molten. The melted wax can then be deposited or trailed on the model to cover a specific, if small, area. It is small because the wax does not take long to cool and reharden. This wax deposit can be further treated with cold carvers or heated tools. It is probably obvious by now that depositing melted wax on the same section of a pattern makes it possible to build up features higher than other areas of the pattern. This is basically the way beads of wax are created, for which the improvised needle tools are especially useful. The technique calls for heating the tool, picking up a small globule of melted wax, allowing it to cool a bit and then gently setting the wax down on the model's surface. Moving the molten wax in a tiny circle with the tool while it is still warm-to-hot helps to round the bead. With a little practice you should be able to make almost perfectly rounded beads. Their size will depend (*a*) on the size of the needle used, (*b*) on how much wax is picked up at one time, and (*c*) on how often melted wax is applied to the same bead or beads. Figure 53 shows a sample of wax beads built up on a small sheet of wax. The column of beads on the right has small beads built up on larger beads. This is accomplished by waiting until the first bead has hardened and then applying melted wax to it with the same or a smaller needle. If desired, three or more beads can be stacked one on top of the other with this technique. Figure 54 illustrates a ring in wax in which beads are used as part of its surface decoration.

Interest can often be added to a model by producing either regular or irregular openings (negative spaces) in an otherwise unbroken pattern. This is achieved by what can be called the "melt out" or "blow away"

Figure 55.
Brooch pattern with
openings created
by "blow away" method.

process. In this operation, a heated tool is used to melt its way through the model's surface. If the tool is held steady and not moved around, a regularly shaped opening is generally produced. Openings that vary in size and shape are achieved by moving the hot shank of the tool (the part immediately behind the working tip) around in the opening. Very often, after the tool is removed, and due to capillary attraction, a thin skin of wax will cover the opening. To eliminate this, the procedure is to hold this section close to your mouth before the wax hardens and *blow away* the thin membrane of wax. The negative or open sections in the demonstration pattern were created by this method (see Figure 55). Long indentations from the outer edge of a model and extending into its inner area can also be formed this way. In addition, the outer edge of a pattern can be smoothed or refined by running the hot shank of a tool around the outline of the pattern.

At this juncture, it should be noted that the entire surface of a model need not be textured or decorated in any similar way in order for the cast jewelry to be effective. It is well, on occasion, to leave a part of a pattern perfectly plain and smooth so that this untreated section of the cast metal may be buffed and polished to a high shine. The bright gleam of a plain area in juxtaposition to one that is textured can provide a pleasing contrast on the ultimate piece of jewelry. In the demonstration model shown earlier in Figure 51 the part of the pattern that curls over was intentionally left plain for this very purpose. In fact the entire surface of a model may be left untextured regardless of what other treatment is given to its form. The demonstration models in Figures 56 and 57 are illustrative of the points being made. There are no hard and fast rules. Craftsmen must be guided by the jewelry article they are creating and their own personal taste for, and appreciation of, pleasing and interesting jewelry designs. Attention should again be called, however, to the fact that gemstones, including pearls as well as other ornamentations, can be added to the cast jewelry to further enhance its attractiveness. Certain of the demonstration patterns shown so far, as well as others which follow, were prepared with this in mind.

Thus far in the build-up process, we have dealt with wax models basically formed from one piece of sheet wax, but models can be created from several pieces of sheet wax bonded together as in Figure 58. In this dem-

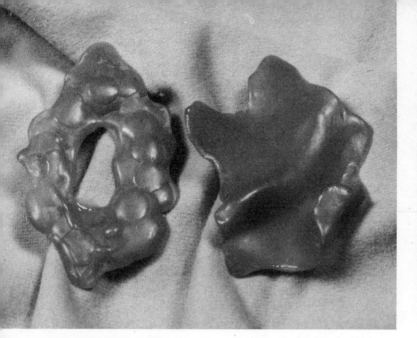

Figure 56. Brooch pattern with perfectly smooth surface.

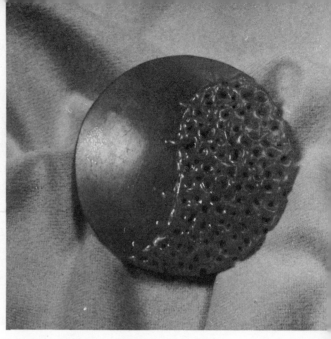

Figure 57. Round pattern is half plain and half textured with small holes.

onstration pattern, the parts were cut from a 20-ga. sheet and then each was textured. The joining was initially done by placing a small bit of sticky wax at the point or points where the pieces were to meet according to the planned design. Sticky wax, however, provides only weak and temporary bond; a stronger, more permanent union is made by the procedure usually referred to as "fusing" or "welding." The fusing (welding) of parts of a model together (temporarily joined by sticky wax or not) is done in two ways. One way is to heat the tip of a tool, such as a needle, and to run it along the place or seam where the parts meet so as to melt a small segment of the meeting parts. A second way is to pick up wax with a heated tool (again a needle will do) and trail it along the place or places where the parts touch. Both methods are often combined for the strongest bond. In either method it is best to make the join where it will not be seen from the front of the jewelry article, providing this is possible. If this is not possible, then the joining must be done with great care so that the initial shape of the parts being united is not spoiled or distorted by the heat of the tool or the wax being applied. Good craftsmanship requires that all sides (back

Figure 58.
Leaf shapes cut
from several wax sheets
and bonded together.

Figure 59. Wax brooch made from round wax wires.

Figure 60. Wax ring made of wires.

as well as front) be given the same loving care and clean workmanship as any single side.

Welding is particularly useful in creating models with wax wires. The demonstration pattern shown in Figure 59 was made from 18-ga. round wax wires. Two pairs of wires were fused together to form its outer perimeter or circle; varying lengths of the same gauge of wire make up the remainder of the pattern. In each case the wires were welded to each other with a heated needle. Then, using a small, heated spatula, molten wax was trailed on each wire in order to eliminate the almost perfectly round appearance of the wires. If this had not been done, the model, when cast, would look as if it had been constructed from 18-ga. metal wire, and this would not be utilizing the lost wax process to its greatest advantage—creating jewelry that could not be produced by the construction process. This same model has a convex shape because the build-up was performed on a convex metal form (plain round door knob). The wax ring shown in Figure 60 was modeled in much the same way except that it was, of course, built up on a ring mandrel.

As demonstrated in Figure 61, wax sheet and wires can be combined in model making. In this pattern, 14-ga. round wires were cut to size based on the sketch that was drawn of the planned jewelry article. Two lengths of wire were cut for each size. Each pair of wires were then placed side by side and welded together. The purpose was to give them greater height when they were turned upright, one above the other, to be welded to the wax sheet. The 20-ga. sheet was cut to shape. This shape—to demonstrate how the portion from which a pendant might be suspended from a chain can be part of the model—included the section on top that was later bent over on itself to provide a place for a jump ring or a slender chain. Each pair of fused wires was warmed, bent to shape by hand or with the help of a smooth tool handle, and then welded to the wax sheet. Needle tools and a small spatula were used to build up the texture around and between the wires; open spaces were then produced in the places shown by the blow-away method.

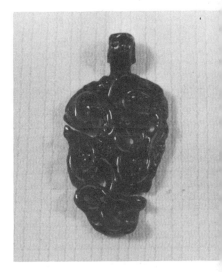

Figure 61.
Wax pendant is made
from sheet wax
and wires.

Figure 62.
All these gemstones
are either
cabochon or baroque
in shape.

As stated before, gemstones and certain other decorative items can be added, if desired, to enhance the attractiveness of many jewelry articles *after* they have been cast in metal. It is also possible to build up bezels and prong settings *in wax* on the model for these same decorative objects so that their settings are cast in metal along with the rest of the pattern. In regard to gemstones, however, it is best to avoid faceted stones since the construction of their settings in metal, let alone wax, is quite difficult for the student craftsman. Basically this leaves gemstones that are either cabochon or baroque (irregular, usually tumbled stones) in shape (see Figure 62). With these, the over-all procedure is to build up the setting around the stone as it rests on its intended place on the model. The first step is to lubricate the stone so that the wax built up around or on it does not stick to it. The second is to build a base for the gemstone that matches the latter's base so that the stone will sit firmly in its ultimate metal setting without rocking up and down. Once the gemstone's base is correctly made, it is a good idea to remove the stone temporarily and to cut out part of the central portion of the wax base, leaving at least ⅛ inch all around (see Figure 63). This is done for three reasons: *(1)* if the stone is transparent or translucent, you will have provided a means for light to pass through the

Figure 63. Cut-out base with cabochon stone
ready to be mounted.

Figure 64. Cabochon stone set with prongs.

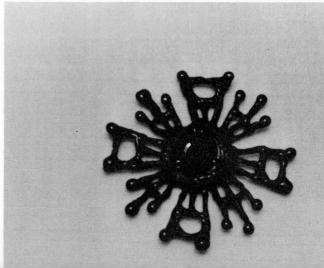

Figure 65. These wax models were
dropped into deep water.

Figure 66. These wax models were
dropped into shallow water.

stone and thus help show off its beauty, (2) you will have reduced the
amount of metal required to make the casting, and (3) you will have provided an opening by which the stone can be pushed out from the completed wax setting by using an appropriate tool.

If the gemstone is to be held by a bezel alone, the latter should not
be made so thick that it will be difficult, if not impossible, after it is cast
to press it over the stone and hold it firmly in place. Even if the stone is to
be held by prongs, it is well (with the stone in its intended position on the
model) to build a low band or bezel around the outer edge (girdle) of the
stone to preclude its slipping later in its metal setting. Prongs can be fashioned from wire or by trailing molten wax up onto the stone. The usual
approach with prong settings is to have their texture match that of the rest
of the model (see Figure 64). It must be emphasized, however, that because molten metal shrinks upon cooling, neither the wax band, bezel nor
the base of the wax prongs should be placed too close to the gemstone's
base. To do so will call for grinding or filing of the inner portions of the
setting in order to have the gemstone fit into its setting comfortably. To
remove the gemstone from a setting where prongs have been used, the model should first be placed in warm water to soften the prongs, and then they
should be gently pried up with a thin knife blade or similar tool (keep dip-
ping in warm water, if necessary, to soften the prongs) until the stone can
easily be pushed out of its setting.

DROP CASTING WAX

Although the drop casting of molten wax cannot, in the strict sense of
the term, be called *creative* model making, no chapter on model making
would be complete without some reference to this "happy accident" method
of producing patterns. The procedure involves melting wax in a porcelain
casserole or enameled pot and dropping small quantities of the liquid wax
into a suitable container of cold water. The resulting shapes will depend on
the amount of wax dropped at one time, and the depth of the water into
which the wax is poured. Figure 65 shows wax models produced when wax
was dropped into cold water 5 inches deep. Figure 66 shows the results with

Figure 67. *Electric wax unit melts wax and keeps it at fixed temperature.*

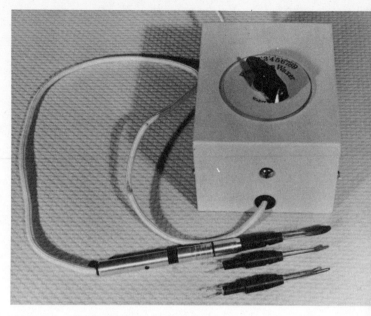

Figure 68. *Electrically heated spatula comes with three different tips.*

ice water ¾-in. deep. In many cases the resulting models are quite heavy or thick in places, which would call for large amounts of metal to fill these places. The way to eliminate this is to carefully carve away the excess wax from the backs of the models so that the wax at these points is reasonably thin. Also keep in mind that two or more of the wax patterns obtained can be joined (welded) together in order to get a more interesting-looking model.

One way to eliminate mistakes from a model—or, indeed, any aspect that displeases you—is to cut or carve the offending item away, a step you can also take to refine aspects that please you. Another way to correct a model or further refine it is to heat a broad-faced tool such as a spatula and use it to melt, pick up and discard the objectionable part, or simply to melt this part down and to smooth the surface. In either case, you can then repair the surface in any way you wish. Completed patterns can be cleaned and given a fairly bright, more finished appearance either by passing them quickly one or more times through a flame, or by rubbing or brushing them carefully with a piece of cotton or a No. 8 or No. 10 camel's-hair brush. For best results, the rubbing or brushing should be done under cold, running water.

Before bringing this chapter to a close, we will digress briefly to mention some of the electric tools available for model making. Though not essential, they do save time and can add to your ability to create unusual jewelry objects. For example, there is a thermostatically-controlled wax unit available (see Figure 67) with several compartments that melts wax and keeps it molten at the temperature you set. Also obtainable is an electrically heated spatula which comes with three differently shaped tips (see Figure 68) that is quite useful in making, repairing and spruing models. This instrument also has a means of controlling the output temperature. And, finally, most casting supply houses offer one or another type of electric wax pen that carries and melts the wax rod you supply it with and at

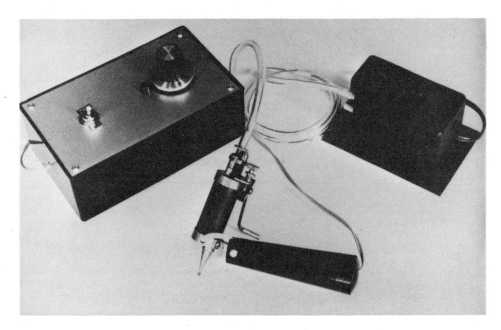

Figure 69.
One type
of electric wax pen.

the temperature you set. Molten wax is dispensed from a point similar to that of a ball-point or felt-tip pen. The wax pen does enable the user to build creative, complicated wax patterns. Two types of these wax pens are shown in Figures 69 and 70, respectively.

Model making with wax—by either the carving or building-up method—is the most intriguing step of all in the creation of jewelry by the lost wax process. It deserves a great deal of practice time to master the few, simple skills involved. Through humble and not very imposing-looking wax you can find an almost perfect means of determining the extent of your originality, your imagination, your artistic ability. And, in addition, you will also have found a fascinating and rewarding way to express yourself as an individual.

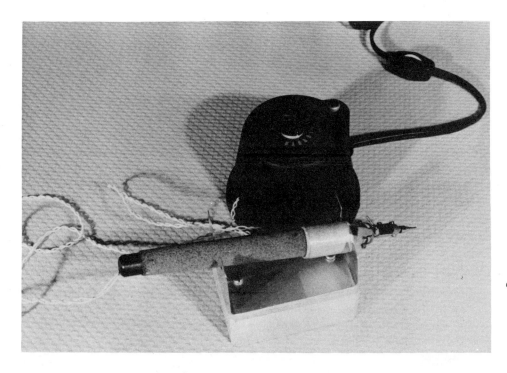

Figure 70.
Another type
of electric wax pen.

Chapter Five

SPRUING THE MODEL

In this and the following three chapters, basic procedures will be detailed that are involved in centrifugal casting, the method used by most craftsmen. Finally, there is a chapter on other modes of casting. Since the information in these chapters is largely applicable to all modes of casting, however, the author decided that the most logical approach would be to describe, first, what is common to all modes, and then to indicate where and how the other modes differ.

WHAT SPRUING IS

Although spruing is mainly a mechanical procedure in the lost wax process (as are investing, burnout and casting), it and the others are still important steps in the production of satisfactory metal castings. Spruing is the step in which wax wires, called "sprues," are attached to models to perform certain significant functions:

1. Their job is to firmly support models in the most appropriate investing and casting positions.
2. They provide pathways in the investment, after they are melted out,
   — through which all the wax of the models may escape from its place in the investment (the mold), and
   — through which molten metal may enter the mold.

Figure 71.
Rubber sprue bases come
in many sizes.

3. They provide space in the passageways for a reservoir of molten metal upon which the metal cast into the mold can draw in order to fill any unfilled spaces as it cools and shrinks in size.

WHAT IS NEEDED

Before getting down to the how-to of spruing, let us examine the equipment used in this step. First, there are the sprue bases, also called "sprue formers" (see Figure 71), upon which the models are mounted by means of sprues. Sprue bases are available in rubber or metal, with the rubber being the preferred type for casting jewelry. The rubber bases come in different diameters corresponding to the sizes of the investment flasks (see Figure 72), also termed "investment rings," into which they are designed to fit snugly as shown in Figure 73. This snug fit is an advantage over the metal kind which requires that a substantial amount of sticky wax be placed around the base of the flask where it meets the sprue base so as to keep the investment, while still in its fluid state, from running out. Note in Figure 71 that the sprue bases are available with either a conically-shaped

Figure 72. A variety of investment flasks.   *Figure 73. Investment flasks fitted into sprue bases.*

center or a depressed circular center. The base with the conical center has a hole through it which should be filled with wax, as should the space of the depressed center. Either type of base is acceptable, except that as a rule no more than two or possibly three small patterns (e.g., rings, tie tacks, cuff links, etc.) may be mounted at one time on the base with the conical center for simultaneous casting. More can be attached to the base with the depressed center. Beginning casters should cast one model at a time until they become thoroughly familiar with the spruing and casting procedures.

Investment flasks, which are the containers into which the investment is poured to totally encase the model, are made of brass tubing or stainless steel tubing, with the latter being the recommended type. The dimensions of flasks will vary to some degree from one manufacturer to another, but they are generally made in these sizes:

TABLE II
DIMENSIONS OF INVESTMENT FLASKS

HEIGHT (inches)		OUTSIDE DIAMETER (inches)
1½	×	1¼
1⅝	×	1¾
2⅜	×	2½
2½	×	3½

Flasks are made in much larger dimensions, but flasks roughly the size of the last three in the above list are the most useful for novice casters, particularly if they are interested in centrifugal casting. Because dimensions of flasks and rubber sprue bases may vary, it is a good idea to get these items from the same supplier to ensure a snug fit between the two. Otherwise, should you buy a rubber base that does not fit its matching flask properly, you will have to use sticky wax to contain the moist investment in the flask.

SPRUING GUIDELINES

Sprue wires—which are generally made of soft, red wax—are available in 6-ga., 8-ga. and 10-ga. diameters. It is impossible to set down hard and fast rules that can be followed in determining the exact size and number of sprues to attach to any one model. The best that can be done is to provide some general guidelines. One rule has it that—in behalf of a solid (nonporous) and complete casting—the size, shape and mass (bulk) of a model has a direct bearing on the size (diameter) and number of sprues that should be attached to a model. A porous casting is one that has small holes in it due to the air and gases entrapped in the casting because sufficient molten metal did not reach the mold to drive them out. An incomplete casting is one that does not have all the details the pattern had, often because sufficient molten metal did not reach the mold to produce them. Therefore the size of the sprue or sprues is important because, as the molten metal flows through the passageways left behind by the burned-out ("lost") sprues, some of it will begin to solidify on the walls of these tunnels. Where the walls are too narrow, the passageways can become clogged, resulting in a porous and/or incomplete casting. The number of sprues is also important because there should be enough passageways to the mold to ensure that sufficient molten metal reaches every part of the mold. Stated another way, the size and number of sprues for a model must be such that molten metal not only fills the mold, but as the metal begins to solidify and shrink, there must be additional metal available in the passageways to draw upon so as to keep the shrinkage and porosity down to the barest minimum.

The above guidelines lead to others. For example, sprues should be kept short so that the molten metal has the shortest feasible distance to travel to reach the mold. The shorter the distance, obviously, the less chance of the metal solidifying before it reaches its destination. Sprues should also be kept as straight and as smooth as possible so that the metal can get to the mold with the least amount of agitation. Sharp corners or bends in sprues create turbulence in the molten metal which, in turn, can cause it to entrap air and gases that produce porous and incomplete castings. Abrupt turns can also cause the molten metal to break off pieces of the investment that, if carried to the mold, can become embedded in the casting. The result will be a casting failure. There are still other guidelines which can best be delineated by providing illustrations and explanations of what they are in this next section.

THE HOW-TO OF PATTERN SPRUING AND MOUNTING

As a first step, select the most suitable flask and its companion sprue base. The size of the flask you will select is determined by the over-all dimensions of your model. As shown in Figure 74, when a wax pattern is sprued and centered inside a flask, its side extremities should be no closer than ⅜ of an inch from the inner wall of the flask, and its top section should

Figure 74.
Wax model's dimensions
dictate size
of flask selected.

Figure 75.
Sprued plain shank ring,
with button.

Figure 76.
Ring with textured shank
has three sprues
and button.

be no closer than ½ inch from the top of the flask. This is to ensure that there will be investment of sufficient thickness on the sides and top of the mold so that the molten metal—which enters the mold under considerable pressure—will not break through the investment and thus spoil a casting. On the other hand, using a flask that is larger than necessary is uneconomical since it will require a larger amount of investment to fill it and more heat to reach every part of the mold in order to burn the wax out.

In spruing any model, it should be born in mind that every wax sprue will be replaced by metal after the burnout and casting steps have taken place. This metal is then cut off the casting, and all evidence of where it was joined to the casting is removed (how this is done will be explained in a later chapter). This fact has a definite bearing in deciding not only where to place a sprue (or sprues) but also on how many sprues should be used. In the case of a ring with a plain shank and not very bulky body, the usual procedure is to attach one main sprue of a suitable size to the shank (see Figure 75). One way to do this is to place a bit of sticky wax on the shank and tack the sprue wire to this. Then, using a heated spatula or needle, the union is made firmer and more secure with additional wax by welding the sprue and shank together to prevent their separation during the investment stage which, as you will learn, involves a certain amount of vibration. Note that where the sprue and shank meet, the junction is flared all around to produce a fillet of wax. This helps the molten metal make the turns required to reach every part of the mold, and is a procedure followed wherever a sprue is attached to a model. The sprue is fixed to the wax of the sprue base with sticky wax and then welded as before. A button of wax about ⅜ inch in diameter is made as close to the model as is practical. Upon burnout and casting, a reservoir of molten metal replaces this button upon which the metal in the mold can "feed" to complete the casting.

When a ring has a textured shank, it is better to use more and thinner sprues, attached to the pattern as shown in Figure 76, in order to preserve the texture of the ring's shank. The same procedure applies to rings whose main portion, or body, is large and bulky, whether or not the shank is plain. Another way to sprue up a ring of the latter type is illustrated in Figure 77. In all instances, the sprues are attached to the model and to the sprue base in precisely the same way (with fillets and buttons).

Up to this point, rings have been used to establish certain spruing criteria only as a matter of convenience. The same principles apply to other relatively small, generally lightweight, jewelry items such as earrings, cuff links, tie-tacks, parts of a link bracelet, and the like. The same over-all guidelines also have relevance to the usually larger and heavier jewelry objects such as pendants and brooches, with a few variations added. Large, solid objects require, as a rule, at least two main sprues to make certain that enough molten metal gets to the mold to complete the pattern (see Figure 78). Note that the pattern is mounted at an angle to the base. This is done for two reasons. One is to avoid having the molten metal enter and strike a flat surface of the mold where it could (being under pressure) damage the mold and destroy detail. Mounted at a slant, the molten metal will merely give the roof of the mold a glancing blow. Another reason is

Figure 77. Ring, all textured, has heavy sprue
inside and thinner sprue to shank.

Figure 78. Heavy wax model is sprued at
slant with two main sprues.

that the air and water in the investment have a tendency, before burnout, to collect as bubbles on the flat surfaces of the model, which are then reproduced as metal beads on the casting. When such a model is sprued in a tilted position, the bubbles will—under the recommended investing techniques described later—tend to flow upward and away from the model's surfaces.

If a jewelry model has two heavy portions separated by a lighter, smaller portion, one main sprue should be attached to each heavy portion with a thinner sprue going to the lighter portion as shown in Figure 79. In the case where a pattern has a heavy, central part from which lighter parts diverge outward in a variety of directions, the main sprue should go to the heavy portion with thinner sprues going to the diverging sections as needed (see Figure 80). Thin sprues should be attached to a section of a mold that is made up of thin wax wires. If the regular 10-ga. red sprue wire is too thick, a 14-ga. green wax wire may be used instead. When an entire model consists of thin wax wires, and when a thick sprue (or sprues) would cover or obliterate parts of the pattern detail, a number of thin

Figure 79. This model has two heavy sections
with lighter section between.

Figure 80. Sprued model with heavy section
and diverging lighter sections.

Figure 81.
Model made of
thin wax wires has
many thin sprues.

sprues must be strategically placed to guarantee a complete casting as in Figure 81.

MULTIPLE SPRUING

Two or more smaller-sized models can be mounted to a sprue base for simultaneous casting, using one or more main sprues for the models (see Figure 82). The techniques for multiple spruing are the same, over all, as for spruing a single pattern. The distances of the outer edges of the models to the flask's inner walls (3/8 inch) and to the top of the flask (1/2 inch) are still maintained. A distance, however, of at least 1/4 inch should be left between the outer edges of each model and those on either side of it. Perhaps the most important consideration is that which concerns

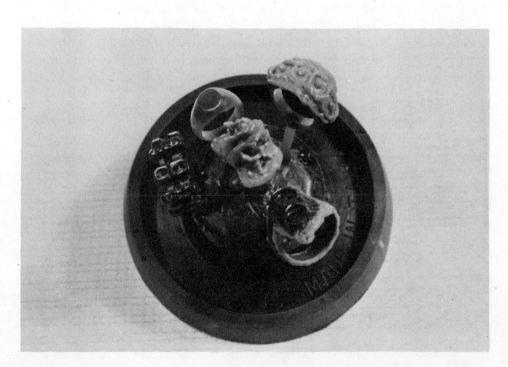

Figure 82.
Several small models
mounted for
simultaneous casting.

the total volume or weight of the metal that will be required for the casting. In the next section, we will consider the methods used to determine the amount of metal that will be needed to replace, after burnout, all the wax of the model, plus that of the sprue or sprues and the button. In centrifugal casting, the metal to be cast is melted in a crucible, and the largest amount of metal that can be melted at one time will depend on the largest size of crucible your casting machine can handle without having the molten metal spill out of the crucible. Let us say that three troy ounces is this maximum quantity. If the amount of metal required to produce a single-sprued or mutiple-sprued casting is *over* three troy ounces, you will not be able to make a successful casting. Thus, if you plan to go into centrifugal casting, it is wise to buy at the outset the machine with the largest casting capacity you can afford.

DETERMINING THE AMOUNT OF METAL FOR A CASTING

There are two methods of doing this. In both, you must include the pattern and its entire sprue system in making the determination. One method (economical but it works, unfortunately, only with small models) is based on water displacement. For this method, you will need a graduate two thirds full of water, plus a length of thin wire. Use a sharp knife or razor blade to carefully cut the sprue system and the model it supports away from the sprue base. Loop a thin wire around a convenient place on the wax and submerge all the wax into the graduate as shown in Figure 83. After noting the level of the water in the graduate, remove the wax. Now place sufficient metal of the kind you plan to cast in the graduate to raise the water level to that which you previously noted. The au-

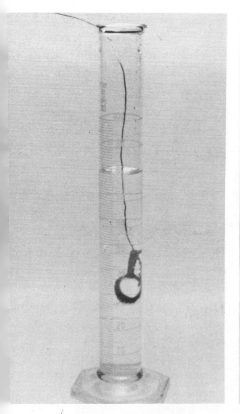
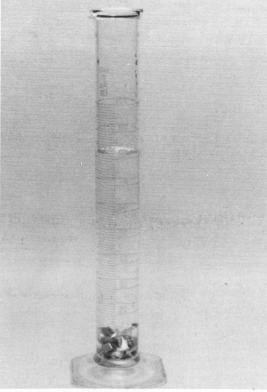

Figure 83.
Model suspended in
water (left), *replaced*
with metal (right).

thor recommends adding about 10 per cent more metal that will, upon casting, provide additional weight to help drive the molten metal through the passageways and into the mold. Dry the wax gently and reweld it back to its original position on the sprue base.

A graduate with a wide mouth and tapered body is also available which will accept larger volumes of wax than the graduate with straight sides. Although the author has never used one, he questions whether the change in water level would be visible enough to make a determination. This would especially apply to small models with small sprue systems.

The second method (which is much more accurate and can handle patterns and sprue systems of almost any reasonable size, including multiple-sprued patterns) employs a scale such as that shown in Figure 84, or another one known as a triple beam scale. These scales usually measure weights in grams, down to tenths and hundredths of a gram. *Note*: Household scales do not provide such fine measurements, nor are they accurate enough for the purpose. The pattern and sprue system is removed from the sprue base as before and weighed. This weight is then multiplied by the specific gravity of the metal to be cast:

TABLE III
SPECIFIC GRAVITY OF METALS USED IN JEWELRY CASTING

gold—18K		gold—10K	
green	15.90	red	11.59
yellow	15.58	yellow	11.57
red	15.18	white	11.07
white	14.64	green	11.03
—14K			
green	14.20	sterling silver	10.46
red	13.26	bronze	9.00
yellow	13.07	brass	8.50
white	12.61	pewter (approx.)	7.65

Figure 84.
Balance scale measures
in grams.

Thus, if a model and its sprue system weighs 5.2 grams and is to be cast in sterling silver, which has a specific gravity of 10.46, multiplying 10.46 by 5.2 determines that approximately 54.4 grams of metal will be needed for the casting. To this, the author again recommends adding another 10 per cent to provide additional metal for the same reason as before. Multiplying 54.4 by .10 gives about 5.5. Thus 5.5 grams of metal should be added. This amount added to 54.4 establishes that 59.9 or 60 grams of metal is to be weighed out.

Although the scales suggested for the specific gravity method are rather expensive, they are also useful for measuring the amount of investment powder needed for different sizes of flasks. On the other hand, any accurate balance scale—perhaps one you can devise for yourself—with a set of gram weights will work just as well.

Chapter Six

INVESTING
THE MODEL

WHAT IS REQUIRED

In order to prepare a model for investing, several things are necessary. Once a model is properly sprued to an appropriate size of sprue base, the next step is to clean it so as to remove any dust, oil (such as that from your fingers) or loose particles of wax that may be clinging to the pattern. A 50-50 mixture of tincture of green soap and hydrogen peroxide (shaken well before each application) applied with a soft camel's-hair brush to all the sprued wax will clean it and also impart a bright sheen to the wax. The soapy residue should be rinsed off with cold water, and the wax carefully and thoroughly dried with a clean paper towel or allowed to air dry.

Wax is a substance that has a characteristic, referred to as "surface tension," which causes it to reject certain liquids such as water. Yet the investment material used to encase a model is sold in powder form which must be mixed with water if it is to serve its purpose. Before it hardens, this water and powder mixture is called "investment slurry." If the investment slurry is to completely and smoothly enclose every portion of a wax model and its sprue system, the surface tension of the wax must be considerably reduced or else air bubbles trapped between the investment and the wax will appear on the casting as unplanned and unwanted metal beads or granules. There are surface tension reducers (also known as wetting agents, debubblizers, de-bubblers, bubble removers) that are commercially available under various trade names. The surface tension reducer is applied to all the sprued wax with a soft camel's-hair brush and allowed to air-dry after making certain that no bubbles of it are adhering to the wax.

Investment powder, a specially compounded casting material, withstands extreme heating, cooling and pressure without cracking or distorting. It is manufactured by various companies and sold by jewelry casting supply houses in packaged amounts ranging from 5, 10, 25 to 100 pounds. These powders, even when made by the same company, can vary in their water-to-powder ratios or proportions; namely, the prescribed amount of water to be mixed with a designated amount of powder to produce an investment slurry that will, in turn, produce the best casting results. This ratio, whatever it may be, must be adhered to as closely as possible to achieve the best results. An investment that is too thin (watery) will be weak and unable to withstand the heat and shock to which it is subjected in the burnout and casting steps. One that is too thick may not flow readily enough to encase all the fine details designed in the model. This leads to an important fact: All investment powders are hydrates—that is, they readily mix with water, including that which exists in the air as water vapor. Over a period of time, absorption of moisture from the air will add to the weight of the powder through mechanical change. This, in turn, will have an effect on the required water-to-powder ratio. For this reason—and regardless of how well you store it—it is well to buy no more powder than you will use in a comparatively short period of time.

The water to be mixed with the investment powder should be at a temperature of 70 to 72 degrees Fahrenheit. Water colder than this will cause the investment to set (harden) more slowly than is desired; warmer water, on the other hand, will cause it to set more quickly than it should. An inexpensive thermometer such as used by amateur photographers who develop their own pictures is good enough to determine water temperatures. For best results, you should draw the water and let it stand for at least an hour before you mix it with the powder. By doing so, and if the room temperature is within the indicated degrees, the drawn water will not only be at the right temperature but it will also contain less air than water drawn from the faucet at the time the mix is made. This is a plus factor since the less air introduced into the investment slurry, the less chance there is of metal granules being produced on the casting.

In discussing the measurement of water and powder and the equipment generally used, it must be borne in mind that the *total* amount of each ingredient will be based on two factors: the prescribed water-to-powder ratio and the size of the flask to be filled. The second factor will be explored in some detail later. For now, what follows is primarily an explanation of the equipment used and how each is used in making the necessary measurements.

1. The simplest and most accurate way to measure the required amount of water is to have a graduate calibrated in cubic centimeters (cc.) or milliliters (ml.). Water requirements are usually given in cc. (1 cc. water = 1

ml. water). It is also possible to weigh out the water needed, using an accurate scale that weighs in grams or in avoirdupois ounces and pounds. First, weigh the container into which you will place the water, then add the required quantity of water based on the following relationships:

1 cc. of water weighs 1 gram
1 gram = .035 ounce avoirdupois

With a scale that weighs in grams, if the amount of water needed is, say, 40 cc., then all you do is add 40 grams of water to the weight of your container. With a scale that weighs in ounces, your formula is 40 x .035 = 1-2/5 ounces. If your container weighs 5-7/10 ounces, then your total weight should come to 7-1/10 ounces. Employing an eyedropper to drop water into the container is helpful in approximating the decimal portion of a weight. Note the weight of the container and set it aside so that you do not have to weigh it each time you use it.

2. In a prescribed water-to-powder ratio, the amount of powder is normally stated in grams. If you have a scale that weighs in grams, you are immediately in business. Simply weigh the container into which you will place the powder and add the required amount of powder. Use of an avoirdupois scale, however, will require a little simple arithmetic, using the 1 gram = .035 ounce avoirdupois relationship. Thus, if the amount of powder required to a fill a flask is, say, 100 grams, your formula is 100 x .035 = 3-1/2 ounces. And if your container weighs 2-1/2 ounces, then the total weight should come to 6 ounces. A spoon or small plastic or metal scoop is useful for transferring the powder from its storage container to the container being used on the scale. Again, note the weight of this latter container and set it aside for future use.

3. The measuring equipment and methods described above achieve the water-to-powder ratio which the manufacturer of an investment powder recommends. There is, however, a method used by sculptors who work with plaster that, with a slight deviation, can be used by casters who do not have a graduate or a scale. The procedure yields rather good results with models that are not too complex or detailed and where the casting need not be too precise. In mixing the plaster, the sculptor places the quantity of water into a container that he has learned from experience is needed to make up a batch that will not harden before he has time to use the mix. He then sprinkles plaster powder all over the surface of the water, allowing the powder to settle down to the bottom. He continues sprinkling until the powder reaches every part of the water's surface. It is at this moment, and not before, that he mixes the water and powder together. For our purpose here, the deviation from this procedure is to have the sprue base with its sprued model tightly fitted together with its matching flask. You then completely fill the flask with water of the right temperature and pour the water into one of the larger mixing bowls recommended in the next section. The rest of the procedure is exactly the same as that which the sculptor follows.

Although any pan, dish or similar utensil that will not absorb water can be employed for mixing the investment slurry, most casters use flexible

Figure 85.
Two bowls and spatula
or knife are
needed for mixing
investment.

rubber bowls specifically made for this purpose (see Figure 85). The advantage of these bowls is that they are easy to clean, particularly when the investment left in them hardens. Merely squeezing the bowl's sides breaks the investment loose for quick disposal. Two bowls are generally needed for reasons to be explained later—one bowl about 3 to 4 inches in diameter and one about 5 to 6 inches in diameter. Adequate substitutes for these bowls can be made from rubber balls (the hollow kind children play with) by cutting them in half—use one each of the suggested diameters. Having mentioned the disposal of investment, we might also stress that as little investment as possible—in slurry or in hardened form—should be washed down the drain because in time this material can clog the drain. It is better to let the investment harden on the tools and equipment and carefully break or scrape it off into a waste receptacle.

A spatula with a sturdy blade and dull edges that will not cut the mixing bowls is the usual mixing implement. A dull table knife is a worthy substitute for the spatula. Both are shown in Figure 85.

Figure 86.
One common type
of electric vibrator.

No matter how carefully it is done, some air will be blended into the investment slurry in the form of air bubbles at the time it is being mixed, as well as when the mixture is being poured into the flask to encase the model. If these air bubbles are not removed, they will tend to collect on the pattern only to be cast in the form of granules as mentioned before. Therefore, some type of device is needed to expel these bubbles from the mix and the invested flask by causing them to rise to the top surface of the investment slurry where they will usually burst and rejoin the outside air. Figure 86 illustrates one of the less expensive, electrically operated vibrators that are commercially available. This vibrator can be set so that its platform vibrates at one of the three speeds indicated on the machine as low, medium and high. Although not so good as a commercial vibrator, certain woodworking power tools—such as an electric sander, a portable saber saw or a regular jigsaw—also can be used to produce the necessary vibrations. The sander (without sandpaper) or the saber saw (without a saw blade) can be mounted upside down in a vise. The shoe plate of these machines becomes the platform on which the vibration procedure takes place. As for the jigsaw, the machine's table is the platform. As a last resort you can place a wood board ¾ in. x 6 in. x 18 in., or thereabouts, on a workbench or table top and strike it lightly, rapidly and repeatedly with a wood, rawhide, plastic or rubber mallet. This improvisation will require the aid of a second person to do the rapping since your hands will be busy doing other things. You may think up still other ways to produce vibrations after you have read the next section on how the vibrations are used to attain the desired casting results.

LINING THE FLASK

Before going into the procedure, it should be noted that there is some difference of opinion among casters as to whether or not a flask should be lined with what is called "asbestos sheet" or "asbestos paper." The asbestos sheet, sold by most casting supply firms, is 1/16-in. thick and is used to cover most of the inside wall of a flask. Those who favor its use claim that by acting as a cushion it enables the investment to expand without cracking during the burnout step, and that after the casting step it greatly aids in removing both the casting and the old investment from a flask. Those opposed argue that it is an unnecessary procedure and additional expense. The author has cast flasks with and without an asbestos liner and goes along with those who support its use, if only because he has found that the liner does make it easier both to remove a casting from a flask and to clean the flask for its next employment.

To line a flask, a strip ¼ in. *less* than the height of the flask is cut from the sheet. The length of the strip is determined by wrapping it around the outside of the flask and marking with a pencil where it meets its free end and then cutting if off about ¼ in. *less* than this measurement. The strip is then moistened on both sides by patting it with fingers wetted in water. The objective is to dampen the strip thoroughly, but not to get it dripping wet. It is then gently patted against the inside wall of the flask so that its edges are each ⅛ in. from the ends of the flask and one end overlaps the other by ⅛ to ¼ in. as shown in Figure 87. The reason for having ⅛ in. of

Figure 87.
Flask lined with
asbestos paper.

the flask's metal exposed at the top and bottom is to provide metal spaces on which the investment can secure or "key" itself so that it will not be moved or dislodged from the flask during the burnout or casting steps.

THE HOW-TO OF MIXING INVESTMENT AND INVESTING

The following conditions must be met *before* you proceed to mix the investment slurry: *(a)* the pattern must be correctly and securely sprued to an appropriate size of sprue base, *(b)* it must have been cleaned and painted with surface-tension reducer which has air-dried, *(c)* you have a clean flask that fits the sprue base, *(d)* you know the prescribed water-to-powder ratio of your investment, and *(e)* you know how much investment slurry is needed to fill the flask completely.

This last condition can be a problem, for the amount of slurry to be mixed will vary with the size of the flask being utilized, and, as was noted, flasks are not all made in standard sizes. In addition, while casting supply catalogs list the dimensions of each flask offered for sale, they, unfortunately, do not give any indication as to its capacity in terms of investment slurry. Nor are those who sell them any more helpful. This makes it difficult to give precise figures of capacity for the flask or flasks you have or may obtain. Yet the correct practice in investing a model is to mix sufficient slurry of the recommended water-to-powder ratio to fill a flask *in one operation* almost to, or even to, slightly overflowing. It is wrong practice to fill a flask only part way and then stop to mix more investment in order to fill the flask completely because this can result in an unsatisfactory casting. On the other hand, it is an uneconomical procedure to mix so much slurry that a substantial part of it is left over and has to be thrown away.

In the author's experience, there are several approaches to the problem:

1. Use the modified sculptor's method of preparing a mix described earlier.

2. Experiment by mixing a batch of slurry of the proper water-to-powder ratio, and see if it fills a flask you intend using. If it is too little, mix more in the prescribed proportion; if it is too much, reduce the amount of water and powder proportionately. Be sure to keep track of how much water and powder you use and make a note of your final determination. You can, of course, use this method for each flask you have. Obviously, once you have the correct figures, you will not need to repeat the experiments.

3. The following chart is presented because it should help anyone who has any flasks the same size as the flasks the author uses most often. If your flask varies only to a slight degree from a given size, you can still use the chart's figures because very small variations will have little effect on the investment's quality. The figures are computed on the 40cc./100 grams investment powder the author uses.

At this juncture, two important points should be stressed: *(1)* in mixing a slurry, *always add the powder to the water* a small amount at a time, and *(2)* most investment slurries have a *total "working time" of about nine minutes*. This time starts when you begin adding the powder to the water, and ends when the flask is completely filled with investment. Ideally, the entire

TABLE IV
CAPACITY OF FLASKS

FLASK SIZE			WATER		POWDER	
Height (in.)	Diameter (in.)	CC.	Ounces Avoir.	Grams	Ounces Avoir.
1-1/2	× 1-1/4	20	7/10	50	1-3/4
1-5/8	× 1-3/4	40	1-2/5	100	3-1/2
2-3/8	× 2-1/2	90	3-1/5	225	8
2-1/2	× 3-1/2	180	6-3/10	450	15-3/4

investment time should take approximately nine minutes, of which about three to four minutes should be devoted to mixing the slurry to ensure that every particle of powder has absorbed its assigned amount of water. The result will be a better and smoother casting. Going beyond the nine minutes, on the other hand, is a risky business because the investment can harden to such an extent that you will experience difficulty in having it flow so as to totally encase the pattern.

If you do not have a vibrating device of any kind, or if the model you are investing is very intricate and detailed, the recommended practice is to paint the model with investment applied with a soft camel's-hair brush. Since several actions in investing a model occur more or less at the same time, including those that take place when some form of mechanical vibration is available, these actions have been broken down step-by-step in an effort to cover them without causing confusion. If you are not painting the model, you can start with Step 2.

STEP 1. In painting a model for whatever reason, measure out the required amount of water and place it in the small rubber bowl. Measure out the requisite amount of powder and set it aside. The quantity of each will depend on the size of the model. With a 40 cc./100 grams investment, you might mix 10 cc. of water with 25 grams of powder for a small model, 20 cc. of water with 50 grams of powder for a medium-sized model or 30 cc. of water with 75 grams of powder for a large-sized model. It is up to you to decide on how much slurry you will need to cover all the wax to a depth of from 1/8 to 1/4 in., the recommended practice.

STEP 2. Measure out the amount of water and powder needed to fill the flask you are using. Place the water in the large mixing bowl. If you are painting the model, set both the water and powder aside without mixing until the painting is done. If you are not painting the pattern, fasten the flask to the sprue base and proceed to Step 4.

STEP 3. To paint a pattern, add the powder to the water set aside for this purpose and mix for the recommended period of time. If you have a vibration device, cushion the sprue base in one hand, as demonstrated in Figure 88, while you paint the model. The vibrations should be at a low rate. With or without a vibration device, do not apply the slurry by dabbing it on the pattern with the brush. Rath-

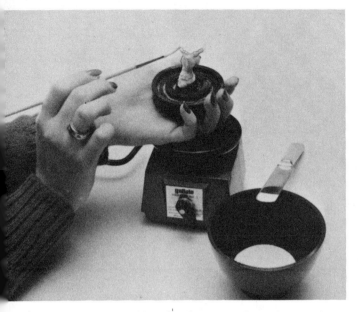

Figure 88. *Sprue base is cushioned in one hand while painting model.*

Figure 89. *Hand cushions sprue base from vibrator while pouring slurry.*

er have the brush push the investment ahead of itself on the wax, which helps avoid air entrapment. Make certain that all the pattern's crevices, undercuts and other intricate details are filled and covered with investment. You may have to turn the model in different directions to accomplish this and to cover all the wax with a coat of the recommended thickness. When you have finished painting, attach the flask to the sprue base and quickly proceed to the next step.

STEP 4. Add the powder to the water you measured out to fill the flask and mix for the suggested time. Then, without a vibrating device, jounce the bowl on a flat surface, which helps drive air bubbles out of the investment. Do this for no longer than one minute or until no more bubbles rise to the surface, whichever occurs first. With a vibrating device, hold the bowl down with both hands on the vibrating platform (or on the board) for the same amount of time or until no more bubbles rise to the surface, again whichever takes place first. The vibrations can be at a high rate.

STEP 5. To fill the flask, hold the sprue base and flask at an angle so that you can pour the slurry down the side of the flask rather than over the model, which can result in entrapping air. This is especially important when investing an unpainted model. The suggested procedure enables the investment to drive the air out ahead of itself as it rises in the flask. With a vibrating device, the hand cushions the sprue base at the same angle with the hand resting on the device as shown in Figure 89. The vibrations should be at a medium rate so as not to cause the sprue (or sprues) to separate from the sprue base or the pattern. Once the slurry is past the

Figure 90. With back of hand resting on vibrator, both hands clasp flask.

Figure 91. Paring off excess investment from top of flask.

topmost part of the model, place the sprue base on a flat surface and keep adding slurry until the flask is completely capped with it, even to the point where it runs over a little.

STEP 6. With no vibrating device, jounce the flask lightly as in Step 3 in a last effort to drive out any air bubbles that may still be in the investment. With a vibrating device, rest the flask straight up in the palm of your hand, with the back of this hand resting on the platform and the fingers of both hands clasping the flask as demonstrated in Figure 90. Use a low or medium vibration rate to drive out any remaining air bubbles. Do your utmost to keep slurry from spilling from the flask. Should you lose any, quickly cap the flask with leftover slurry.

The invested flask is now set on a level surface where it will not be disturbed in any way for at least one hour. This is known as the "setting time" during which the investment is setting or hardening. Large flasks may require as much as two hours or more. Any marked disturbance during the setting time could cause the investment to crack at places that could result in a damaged casting. After the suggested setting time, the sprue base may be removed by gently pushing the lip of the sprue base off the flask. When you feel that the base is free to turn, hold it in one hand and turn the flask with the other to break the model's sprue (or sprues) away from the wax in the base. With the base and flask apart, you will be able to see the sprue wax in the cavity of the flask.

The next task is to clean the flask of any investment that may have hardened on its side or edges. Use a knife to scrape this off. For the flask to be properly seated in the casting equipment, the investment on the top and bottom of the flask must be perfectly level with the flask's top and bottom edges. When it is not, the investment should be shaved flat and level with them. This is best accomplished by using a sharp knife whose blade is longer than the diameter of the flask and by letting the blade ride on the flask's edges as it slices off the excess investment (see Figure 91).

Also, it is essential that you closely examine the cavity left in the investment by the sprue base to make certain that no loose bits of hardened investment are present there. This is the area through which the molten metal will enter the passageways leading to the mold in the casting step. Unless removed by brushing them out with a small brush or a finger, these particles may be carried by the liquid metal either into the passageways where they could become a roadblock or into the mold to become embedded in the cast metal. Either way the result would be an imperfect casting.

BALANCING THE CASTING MACHINE

The next major step in the lost wax process is the elimination (burnout) of the wax encased in the flask. With some types of casting equipment, this step can occur immediately after the flask has been prepared according to the instructions above. In centrifugal casting, however, an action must be taken *before* burnout because there is no time between the end of the burnout cycle and the time the casting should take place to perform this action. This involves balancing the casting machine. Centrifugal casting machines can differ in a number of ways. Some use an electric motor, others use a heavy-duty spring to rotate an arm on the machine at great speed, thus generating the centrifugal force needed to drive the molten metal from the crucible into a flask. On some machines the arm turns in a vertical plane; on others the arm turns in a horizontal plane. Most craftsmen use the spring-operated machine that turns the arm horizontally. All arms carry a set of weights on one end and a place for a crucible and flask on the other end. The arms can differ, however, in that on some machines the arm is rigidly straight, while other machines have what is termed a "broken" arm in which the part of the arm that carries the crucible and flask is perpendicular to the rest of the arm before centrifugal force is applied (see Figure 92). This part is free to pivot 90 degrees so that when

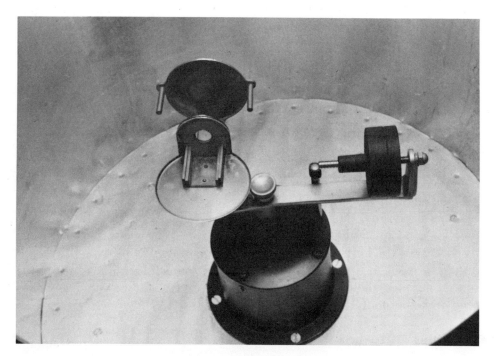

Figure 92.
Casting machine arm,
"broken," without
crucible and flask.

Figure 93.
Casting machine,
arm straight,
with crucible,
cradle, flask and metal.

centrifugal force is applied, it is literally shot forward by this force to line up with the rest of the arm, thus providing additional energy to the centrifugal energy which injects the molten metal into the flask.

Both the straight and broken arms must be balanced if they are to work properly, and if the shaft on which the arms rotate is not to be subjected to uneven wear. With the broken arm, this part is first aligned with the rest of the arm by wedging a thin piece of wood, a piece of cardboard or a match stick in the place where the broken section pivots. With both types of arms, the invested flask with its required cradle, if any (more about this later), is placed up against the metal retaining plate on the arm. The sprue wax in the flask cavity faces the crucible carrier which is designed to move back and forth an inch or so. The proper size of asbestos-lined crucible is set on the crucible carrier, and the carrier is moved up against the flask. The metal measured out earlier to produce the casting is placed in the crucible. The arm, with the load it carries on each end, now appears as illustrated in Figure 93. Then the nut in the center of the arm is loosened so that the arm is free to rock up and down on the shaft's end. The weights on the arm are adjusted until a little tap on either end of the arm causes it to tilt down in the direction of the tap. When this happens, the machine is balanced, the weights are locked together (they are usually designed to do this) and the center nut is tightened. With the broken arm, whatever is holding it in line with the rest of the arm is removed. Note, however, that the machine is balanced *for this one casting only.* Since the weight of a model, flask, investment, crucible and metal to be cast can differ from one casting to the next, the machine must be rebalanced for each individual casting.

You may now remove the flask from the machine and proceed to the burnout step. If, for any reason, you must delay this step for any appreciable length of time, the investment must be kept damp by wrapping the flask in a damp cloth (a Turkish towel serves very well) until you are ready to start the burnout cycle. Dried-out investment will frequently crack during burnout. If an invested flask does dry out, submerge it in water for several minutes, then take it out, dry off the excess surface water and proceed to the burnout.

Chapter Seven

BURNOUT

The burnout step, while quite simple, is nonetheless very important to the achievement of successful castings. It must be done correctly and carefully for it performs several significant functions: (*a*) it eliminates all the water from the investment, which allows the latter to harden completely; (*b*) it eliminates all the wax encased in the investment, including wax residues such as carbon, and (*c*) it brings the flask to the casting temperature that is appropriate for the size of the jewelry article and the specific metal being cast. It is important that you do not start the burnout cycle unless you are ready to carry on through the entire casting step. Starting the cycle, stopping it and allowing the flask to cool, and then reheating the flask will only result in cracked investment and a ruined mold.

WHAT IS NEEDED

Burnout furnaces of two types, gas and electric, are available. Many, if not most, craftsmen use the electric type (see Figure 94). Gas furnaces have a vent on top that permits gas and wax fumes to escape from the furnace chamber. A hood (such as is placed over modern kitchen stoves) should be installed over the vent so that these fumes can be vented to the outside by means of an exhaust fan. Ideally, an electric furnace should be similarly equipped for the same purpose. However, the wax fumes, for the

Figure 94.
Electric furnace.

most part, are not so serious or objectionable that they cannot be allowed to escape into the work area if they cannot conveniently be vented outside. Since these fumes must have some way to exit from the furnace chamber, the simplest procedure is to leave the furnace door slightly ajar during the early stages of burnout until no more smoke is seen leaving the furnace chamber. Should you, by chance, have an enameling or other front-loading kiln (a top-loading ceramic kiln exposes you to too much heat), it can be employed for burnout, provided the chamber floor is covered with a clay shelf or a piece of sheet asbestos so that the wax dripping from the flask will not contaminate the floor. The author has used an enameling kiln for several years without any problem by keeping the chamber's floor, ceiling and walls clean. When purchasing a burnout furnace, there are a number of factors which deserve consideration:

1. CHAMBER DIMENSIONS. The interior dimensions of a furnace can vary in terms of height, width and depth. Selection should depend, primarily, on the size of the largest flask your casting equipment can accept, and the number of flasks you would like, preparatory to casting, to burn out at one time. As over-all guidance, it may be pointed out that most craftsmen use flasks that are no larger than 3½ in. diameter by 4 in. high, and they generally burn out no more than two flasks at one time.

2. PYROMETER AND RHEOSTAT. Although it is possible to obtain a furnace without these devices, it is most desirable to have one equipped with them. A pyrometer is an instrument that measures temperatures by means of a thermocouple. The thermocouple, which is sensitive to heat and heat changes is set into the furnace chamber, and the temperatures it encounters are registered on a dial which is usually calibrated in both centigrade and

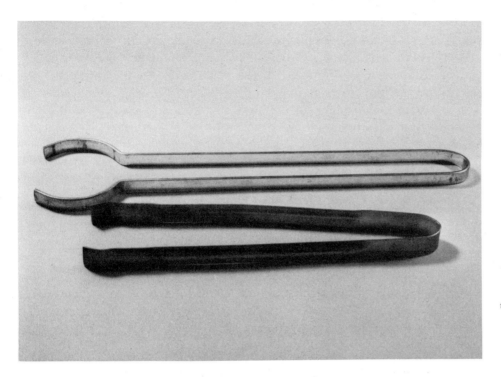

Figure 95.
Tongs are needed
when using burnout furnace.

Fahrenheit degrees. The rheostat is employed to change and control the amount of electric current sent to the coils that heat the chamber—the less current, the lower the temperature; the more, the higher the temperature. Since, during burnout, the temperature in the chamber must be raised as well as reduced to different degrees at rather specific times and held there, it is easy to see the value of having a furnace equipped with a pyrometer and rheostat.

Tongs are required for inserting a flask into the furnace and especially for removing a hot flask from the furnace. Two sizes are shown in Figure 95—the shorter size for handling small flasks, the larger size is for handling both small and large flasks.

To eliminate the wax from a flask, the flask is placed in the furnace sprue hole down. To aid wax burnout, air must be able to circulate under the flask so that oxygen can reach the wax to produce combustion. The invested flask must be set on a support that can withstand high temperatures and that will raise the flask just enough for oxygen to reach the wax. Illustrated in Figure 96 are items that with one exception (the asbestos

Figure 96.
Kiln furniture.

sheet) are available from dealers in metal enameling and ceramic supplies. Starting at the left in the top row is a wire mesh rack with "legs," in the center is a rack that can be placed on any of the objects in the bottom row, and on the right is a ceramic star stilt. On the left in the bottom row are ceramic triangle rods (or pins), in the center are two pieces cut from a soft refractory block and at the right are pieces cut from sheet asbestos. This last item is the simplest solution of all, with the asbestos sheet being available from most lumber dealers.

THE HOW-TO OF BURNOUT

The burnout cycle is conducted in stages. The temperatures at which, along with the period of time, these burnout stages are conducted often differs from one craftsman to another, depending on what each has found to work successfully for him. Craftsmen will also differ about the size of the flask. Below are the burnout stages the author has used with success (the temperatures are Fahrenheit). With a furnace that has a pyrometer and rheostat, the different heats are reached by turning the rheostat up until the suggested temperature is registered on the pyrometer gauge. The rheostat is then adjusted up or down, as needed, until the temperature holds at the desired degree of heat.

TABLE V
BURNOUT STAGES AND TEMPERATURES

	FLASKS UP TO 2½ in. × 2½ in.	FLASKS UP TO 3½ in. × 4 in.
1st stage	1 hour at 300°	1 hour at 300°
2nd stage	1 hour at 600°	2 hours at 600°
3rd stage	1 hour at 1100°	2 hours at 1100°
4th stage	2 hours at 1350°	2–3 hours at 1350°
5th stage	1 hour. Reduce to proper casting temperature	1 hour. Reduce to proper casting temperature

The furnace should be preheated to 300 degrees when the flask is initially placed in the chamber. In the second stage, the wax begins to melt out of the flask while the water in the damp investment begins to turn to steam. These actions increase visibly and more rapidly during the third stage, and you will see steam and smoke produced by the burning wax exiting through the slightly opened door. The main reason for the gradual increase of heat which results in a similar gradual release of steam from the investment is that, if the steam built up very quickly in the investment, the pressure exerted could easily cause cracks. The reason for holding temperatures for the recommended periods of time is based on the fact that the chamber will reach each temperature level much before the center of the flask will. Hence additional time is needed to equalize the temperature inside and outside the flask.

The fourth stage (often referred to as "heat-soaking" the flask) is necessary because as the wax burns out it leaves a carbon residue behind

Figure 97.
Properly burned-out
flask (right);
improperly burned-out
flask (left).

which can be totally eliminated only by subjecting it to higher heat over a period of time. Residue present in the mold can spoil a casting. One way to tell if the residue has been burned out completely is to remove the flask from the furnace with tongs (wear asbestos gloves), and turn it so that you can see the sprue hole and the investment around it. If no wax is burning, and if the investment appears as in the flask on the right in Figure 97 it has had sufficient burnout even if the time suggested for the fourth stage has not been completely taken. If it appears as in the flask on the left, more burnout time is required. Note that the furnace temperature should not exceed 1350 degrees because above that—and certainly above 1450 degrees—the investment begins to break down physically.

The fifth stage requires a special bit of explanation. The purpose in reducing the furnace temperature—and thus of the flask—is to ensure that the cast molten metal does not remain in a liquid state so long that it absorbs gases which can result in a porous casting. The following temperatures are recommended:

TABLE VI
INVESTMENT CASTING TEMPERATURES

Gold	
Thin, lacy jewelry articles	1050° to 1100°
Thick, heavy jewelry articles	800° to 900°
Sterling silver	750° to 850°
Bronze	900° to 1000°
Brass	750° to 800°
Pewter	The flask should be cooled to room temperature (72°)

When the burnout cycle is completed, you are ready to proceed to the casting step.

Chapter Eight

CENTRIFUGAL CASTING

Centrifugal casting machines can be purchased with certain accessories or without them. It is important for you to know that such accessories as crucibles and flask cradles (the curved metal objects on the right in Figure 98) which fit one manufacturer's machine will not necessarily fit another's. It is, therefore, essential that when you add accessories you be absolutely sure they will fit your machine. This warning also includes flasks, since some machines will accept flasks as tall as 4 inches or taller, while others are limited to flasks no higher than 3½ inches. For the most efficient and effective operation of a machine, including personal safety, the following criteria should be met.

1. All centrifugal casting machines are designed to be bolted down to some type of surface. This can be a heavy workbench or a similar weighty and sturdy support. The author—not willing to give up valuable space on his workbench—built a boxlike foundation out of heavy lumber into which he placed several heavy concrete blocks (see Figure 99). While the contrivance can be pushed around the workshop, it stands immovable during the casting process.

2. The surface on which the machine is mounted should be perfectly level. A machine that is not level will have its revolving arm materially slowed down, with a resultant loss of the centrifugal energy needed for a successful casting.

Figure 98.
Centrifugal casting
machine.

3. Because molten metal can, even on infrequent occasions, be thrown out of the crucible when the machine's arm first starts to rotate, it is a good idea to have a protective barrier between your body and the machine. This can be accomplished by mounting the machine inside a metal can such as an old-fashioned washtub or low ash can. The author encircled his machine, as shown in Figure 99, with wide aluminum sheet that is used as flashing on roofs.

WHAT IS NEEDED

Crucibles come in about five sizes, based on the maximum weight in troy ounces of gold that can be melted in them. A crucible that has, for example, a 2½-oz. capacity will also be usable with the same quantity of silver or any other metal used in jewelry casting. It is recommended, how-

Figure 99.
Homemade casting machine
base and protective
metal enclosure.

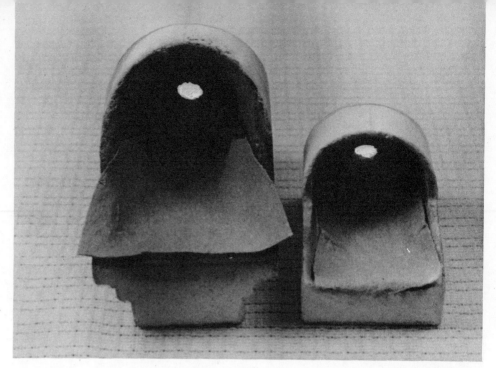

Figure 100.
Two crucibles
with protective liners.

ever, that one crucible be used for gold, another for silver, and still another for the base metals (bronze, brass, pewter).

Asbestos liner, 1/16-in. thick, is needed—the same as that used to line flasks. A piece is cut to line the bottom of a crucible, as shown in Figure 100, so that the metal does not pick up any clay particles of the crucible, and the crucible does not retain any particles of the metal. The cut piece is dampened with water and pressed into place with the fingers. A new liner should be used with each casting. A substitute for this is to melt (see Chapter 1) a borax/boric acid mixture or borax crystals in the crucible in such a way as to glaze its inner surface with the material. These borax substances, it should be recalled, are also used as casting fluxes for all metals except pewter.

Flask cradles, if needed, are generally supplied with the machine. They serve to support the smaller flasks so that the opening in the crucible is aimed (when the burned-out flask is correctly positioned on the machine's arm) directly at the sprue hole(s) in the investment through which the liquid metal enters the passageways and the mold. Large flasks, as a rule, do not require cradles.

A 1- or 2-gallon metal pail half-filled with water is needed, for the purpose that will become clear shortly.

PREPARATORY TO CASTING

During the time that a flask is being burned out, there are several actions that should or can be performed:

1. The metal (except pewter) weighed out for the casting should be cleaned by first heating it with a torch, pickling it in hot pickle and rinsing it in clean water. Dry with a clean cloth or paper towel.

2. Wind the machine (that you balanced earlier) by taking hold of the weighted end of the arm and turning it clockwise three or four full turns, based on the instructions of the machine's manufacturer. The count starts at the point where you have to begin exerting force to turn the arm.

Three complete turns is the usual number. You will have to exert more force as you wind the heavy spring, and it is the swift unwinding of this spring that produces the centrifugal energy. When you have reached the required number of turns, pull up the rubber-tipped stop rod from the machine's base just high enough to permit the arm to rest against it. The recommended casting position is to have the crucible and stop rod on your left and the arm's weights on your right as you face the machine.

3. Place the properly prepared crucible on the crucible carrier and put the cleaned metal in it. Pull the crucible carrier back as far as it will go.

4. If a flask cradle is required for the flask being burned out, install it on the arm in the place designed to hold it. The machine should now appear as in Figure 101.

THE HOW-TO OF CENTRIFUGAL CASTING

Just about the time the flask is reaching the recommended casting temperature for the metal being cast, you can start to melt the metal in the crucible. Sprinkle a little borax flux over the metal (except pewter), which will aid in keeping the metal from oxidizing. Use a flame that is referred to as a "reducing flame" as opposed to one called an "oxidizing flame." A reducing flame is one that does not hiss loudly and that displays a tinge of yellow along with the blue. The flame itself—about 3 to 3½ inches long— has a section that produces less oxidation on the metal. That is the zone immediately ahead of the light blue cone of the flame and extending 1 to 1¼ inches. This deeper blue area is also the hottest part of the flame. Angle

Figure 101. Centrifugal casting machine as it appears when ready to cast.

the torch so that the flame is targeted directly on and over the metal. As the metal shows signs of melting, sprinkle a little more flux on it and turn off the flame.

Now remove the flask from the furnace with tongs and place it on its cradle, if any, with the sprue hole facing the crucible opening. With a gloved hand, push the crucible carrier up tightly against the flask. Holding the torch in your left hand, return to heating the metal with a reducing flame until it begins to shine like a mirror and appears to spin. Continue to heat the metal to ensure that all of it is molten (but not to the point where it begins to boil). Gently jiggling the arm's weighted end with your right hand will make the metal roll around a little if it is completely fluid. If it is, continue holding the flame on the metal, grasp the weighted end of the arm with your right hand and pull it toward you just enough to free the stop rod and have it fall back into its place in the base. Count 1—2—3 and, at precisely the same time, release the machine's arm, raise both arms up from the machine and step back about a foot. Turn off the torch.

If the machine was properly bolted or weighted down and level, and if it was properly balanced, the arm will spin swiftly and smoothly counter-clockwise. Allow it to spin until it stops of its own accord no matter how anxious you are to see how your casting turned out. In the interval, the metal will cool and solidify. When the arm has come to a complete stop, pull the crucible carrier back with a gloved hand, grasp the flask with tongs and submerge it in the pail of water. Swishing the flask around with the tongs serves to bring it constantly into contact with cool water. The investment in the flask will start to break up and out of the flask. Do not try to retrieve your casting until you are sure that the metal is cool enough to handle with bare hands. If the casting has not dropped out of the flask, it may be pushed out with your fingers.

Any investment clinging to the casting can be chipped off with a dull tool. Just be careful not to damage any part of the jewelry object itself. Small particles can be scrubbed off with a stiff bristle brush. A toothbrush is useful in removing investment from hard-to-reach places. Chip off bits of investment that stick to intricate parts of the casting with a suitable tool. All this cleanup—including the flask—can be done with the water in the pail in which the hot flask was immersed.

One way for getting rid of the investment collected in the pail is to let the investment settle until the water above it is almost clear. Then pour off as much clear water as possible into a drain. Continue this procedure until only a little water is left, after which the pail's contents can be disposed of in a plastic bag or in a garbage can itself.

Chapter Nine

OTHER METHODS
OF CASTING

In addition to drop, cuttlefish bone and centrifugal casting, there are other methods you may wish to know about and investigate. Because of the ever-growing interest on the part of an increasing number of people in jewelry casting as a hobby, as an income-producing venture or for many other reasons, more companies are coming forth with a variety of equipment manufactured for this purpose. However, it is not the objective of this chapter to catalog or (with one exception) evaluate the different kinds of casting devices currently on the market. Nor (with one exception) is it our purpose to describe precisely how a casting is made. What we intend is to give you some notion of what is available, the basic principle on which the casting equipment functions, and its over-all cost in relation to a centrifugal casting machine and its accessories.

STEAM PRESSURE CASTING

This is an old process that still has some usefulness for the student of jewelry casting who is content with casting wax models that are not too ambitious—in size or complexity. In this method, steam under pressure is used to supply the energy needed to force the molten metal into the mold cavity. There are one or two low-priced kits offered for sale that cost much less than a centrifugal casting machine and its accessories. But if you have all the supplies and equipment required for creating a model and taking it

Figure 102.
Copper sprue base used
in steamcasting.

through the burnout step, you can probably improvise all else that is needed
to cast the model by the steam pressure process.

Due to where and how the metal to be cast in this process is placed,
a special sprue base must be constructed for reasons that will become
apparent shortly. The first task is to select a flask that you will use with
this method. Do not choose one much larger than about 2½ in. diameter
and 3 in. high, because the steam pressure you will be able to generate
will only be capable of driving a limited amount of liquid metal only a
relatively short distance. Figure 102 shows a sprue base fashioned from
a square piece of soft 20-ga. copper (22 ga. or 24 ga. may be used if it is
malleable). The dimensions of the copper should be such that, when the
flask is centered on the sheet, no part of the flask extends over any edge of
the copper. Find the center of the sheet and indent it lightly with a center
punch. The next job is to raise a dome in the copper. The diameter of the
dome's base should be ½ in. less than the diameter of the selected flask.
Refer to the tools illustrated in Figure 103 with which the dome can be

Figure 103.
These tools will
be useful in raising
dome in copper.

shaped, with every expectation that your imagination will take over from there. The center mark on the copper is used as the central point of the dome. The copper around the dome is kept flat by hammering or malleting it down on a flat surface.

Once the dome is raised, drill a hole in its center with a 1/16-in. (or Number 52 or 53) twist drill bit. Also drill holes for small wood screws in each corner of the copper. Mark the center of a square piece of ¾-in. wood that is ½ in. to ¾ in. wider all around than the domed copper piece and drill a hole through it with the same bit used in making the hole in the copper. Make what can be called a "sprue pin" by cutting a 2-in. piece of stiff 14-ga. wire (brass, copper or other metal) and force it into the hole in the wood block so that only about 1¼ in. extends above what will be the top surface of the wood. You may have to enlarge the hole in the dome slightly in order to be able to place the domed copper on the wood block with the sprue pin protruding through the dome's hole. The pin should extend about ⅝ in. above this opening. Now square the copper piece with the wood block and secure it to the wood with screws. The assembled sprue base should look much like that in Figure 104. The sprue pin will provide the passageway to the mold. The reason for having this passageway so narrow is that the metal for casting is melted in the depression left in the investment by the sprue-base dome. If this passageway were wider, liquid metal could begin to flow down it and solidify long before the major part of the metal was ready to be cast.

Steam pressure producing tool is a high-sounding name for the unassuming homemade implement shown in Figure 105. To make it, select a jar lid or other lid that is large enough to slip easily over an end of the flask you plan using. It should, however, not be so large that a great deal of the steam it is intended to help produce will escape. This lid should also be at least ⅝ in. deep. Drill a hole in the center of the lid and fasten it with a screw to the end of a ¾-in. or 1-in. dowel or piece of discarded broom or mop handle about 8 inches long. Cut circles out of 1/16-in. to 1/4-in. sheet asbestos that fit snugly when pressed inside the lid. Leave about ⅛ in. or a little more of the lid unfilled.

Figure 104.
Assembled steam-casting
sprue base
should look like this.

Figure 105.
Homemade tool for
producing
steam pressure.

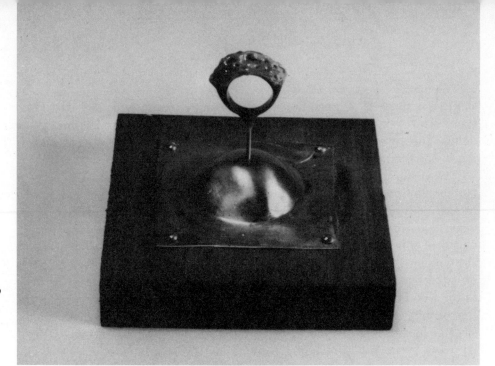

Figure 106.
Model welded to
sprue pin.

The asbestos in the steam pressure producing tool is soaked in a pan of water just prior to the casting step.

The wax model is prepared, and a short length of 10-ga. sprue wire is welded to it. The amount of metal needed to produce the casting is determined, using one of the procedures described earlier. The sprue wire is then welded to the end of the sprue pin (see Figure 106). The wax is cleaned and all bubbles removed. Center the flask on the sprue base and fix it there firmly by placing sticky wax all around its bottom edge. Follow the same investing and burnout actions as before. Prepare the metal for casting. When the flask has been properly burned out, set it on an asbestos pad (sprue hole up), place the metal in the depression and begin to melt it

Figure 107.
Steam pressure producing
tool is removed
from water and placed
on flask.

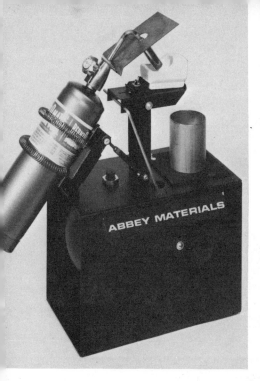

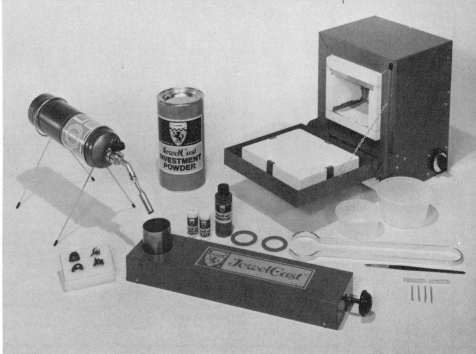

Figure 108. The Mini-Vac
vacuum-assist casting machine.

Figure 108A. The JewelCast vacuum-assist casting
machine comes as a complete kit.

with a reducing flame, adding flux as previously prescribed. Have the
steam pressure tool standing in the pan of water close at hand. When the
metal begins to melt, remove the tool from the pan and shake off any excess
water (see Figure 107). The asbestos should be saturated with water, but
surplus water can cool the metal before it has time to flow down to the
mold. All the metal is melted when it has a mirrorlike surface and appears
to swirl around with small circular movement of the torch. Holding the
flame on the metal, quickly set the tool squarely on top of the flask and
hold it there firmly for 30 to 45 seconds. You will probably hear and see
the steam generated, so be prepared for it. It would be well to have some-
one standing by to take the torch from you and turn it off. Remove the tool
and, when the metal has cooled sufficiently, immerse the flask in a pail of
water and remove the investment from the casting and flask as before. It
is always easier to do this cleanup immediately than to do it after the investment has had time to dry and reharden.

VACUUM-ASSIST CASTING

With this casting method, equipment is used to withdraw the air and
any gases from the burned-out flask (hardened investment is still porous),
thus creating a vacuum in the flask—especially in the passageways and
mold cavity or cavities. An old adage has it that "nature abhors a vacuum,"
and does everything to fill it. In vacuum-assist casting, the vacuum is filled
with molten metal. Figure 108 shows one type of equipment that is available
which creates a vacuum that draws the liquid metal into the flask. Its trade
name is Mini-Vac and its cost is less than that of a centrifugal casting machine. An entire kit is sold under the trade name of JewelCast. It also employs a vacuum in its casting step. See Figure 108A.

There are much more sophisticated vacuum-assist machines available

Figure 109.
Vacuum-assist investing
machine.

that produce better results than any equipment discussed so far, including the centrifugal machine. The only problem is that the cost (higher than the centrifugal machine) may be too much for beginners or, for that matter, many established craftsmen. For those novices and craftsmen, however, who have the funds to expend, the vacuum-assist machines shown are excellent buys. These machines are operated by an electric motor that drives a pump which produces the vacuum.

We must now digress briefly to explain that it is possible to obtain a vacuum-assist machine whose sole function is to eliminate air bubbles from freshly mixed investment (see Figure 109). No vibrating device is needed with this equipment. As soon as the flask is invested, it is placed on the table under the bell jar, the motor is turned on and the pump produces a vacuum in the bell jar which serves to draw the air bubbles out of the investment. The casting may then be done with a centrifugal casting machine or other casting equipment. There are, however, vacuum-assist machines designed to do both the investment and casting jobs. These are shown in Figures 110 and 111. The table and bell jar in each photograph are used for the elimination of air bubbles from a freshly invested flask. (Actually the left half of the machine is a replica of the machine described above.) Then after the flask has been burned out, it is centered, sprue hole up, over the opening in the table on the right. A control on the front of the machine is turned so that the pump now draws the air out of the flask (the bell jar plays no part in this). The metal to be cast is melted in a handled melting

Figure 110. Vacuum-assist investing/casting machine.

Figure 111. Vacuum-assist investing/casting machine.

Figure 110. Vacuum-assist investing/casting machine.

Figure 111. Vacuum-assist investing/casting machine.

dish such as appears in the lower part of Figure 110, and is poured into the flask when the proper amount of vacuum has been reached.

There is a homily heard many times in different forms which is worth following. It goes: "When you buy something, it always pays in the long run to buy the best, regardless of cost." That, of course, is easy to say, but the fact remains that a poor tool or inferior equipment will not last very long, will yield unhappy results and lead to many frustrations. Good tools and well-made equipment will not only last much longer but will help ensure satisfaction with the work plus successful results. And to quote another old chestnut: "Nothing succeeds like success."

Chapter Ten

FINISHING CAST JEWELRY

In the remarks directed to the reader in the opening section of this book, we stated that this book did not plan to go into the how-to of such jewelry-making techniques as sawing, filing, annealing, pickling and others which are covered in our book on jewelry construction, *Jewelry Making as a Hobby.* This chapter, therefore, will deal mainly with the few extra procedures that apply to cast jewelry.

If every step taken to produce the casting was performed carefully and properly, there should not be much finishing to do. If the casting has prongs to hold a gemstone or other added ornament, however, we suggest that you first anneal the article. Cast metal has a tendency to be somewhat brittle, so that when the prongs are moved there is always the chance that one or more of them may break off. Annealing will make the prongs more pliable, and you can place the heated piece in hot pickle. If the casting does not require annealing, it, too, should be placed in hot pickle, which aids in removing the oxides that coat the metal plus as a rule, any tiny bits of investment that may still be clinging to the casting in hard-to-reach places. After pickling, which will leave the metal much brighter, rinse and dry the casting.

The next task is to remove the sprue(s) and sprue button. This can be done with the jeweler's saw or with heavy-duty metal-cutting pliers. Cut the sprue(s) off as close to the jewelry object as you can, being careful

Figure 112.
Pendants made of
centrifugally cast silver,
parts of
which are enameled.

not to cut into the article or scratch or gouge it in any way. The metal cut off can be cast again provided that at least 50 per cent fresh metal (metal not previously cast) is added to it. This is to help replace some of the alloys that may have been burned out of the cast metal when it was melted. File away all evidence of where the sprue(s) was attached to the casting. Dents or scratches that may have gone unnoticed in the wax pattern should also be filed or buffed away. Air bubbles left in the investment may have produced unplanned-for metal beads on the casting despite all you did to prevent it. These can be filed away, or left if you feel they add interest to, or enhance the appearance of, the jewelry. Do all required soldering, including the attachment of findings (if any), before you give the piece its final buffing and polishing. Leave the setting of gemstones or any other added ornamentation to the last.

Figures 112 through 121 illustrate jewelry items made by the author. They were chosen as examples because they were relatively simple to make, and we do not suggest that you copy them. To slavishly duplicate—without adding much that is your own—is to deprive yourself of the great pleasure that can be yours *only* if what you design and create is also yours—something that expresses you as an individual. These pieces are also shown to give you some idea of the variety of jewelry that can be created by casting alone or by combining castings with forms of jewelry fabrication.

Figure 113.
Cuff links and tie tack.
Centrifugally cast
14K gold "frames" into which
old U.S. coins are set.

Figure 114. Pendant/pin.
Centrifugally cast silver "frame"
with bezel into
which enameled silver is
set as one would
set a cabochon-shaped gemstone.

Figure 115. Silver pendant, shown earlier in Chapter 1. Here a blue baroque pearl
and a faceted synthetic sapphire have been added.

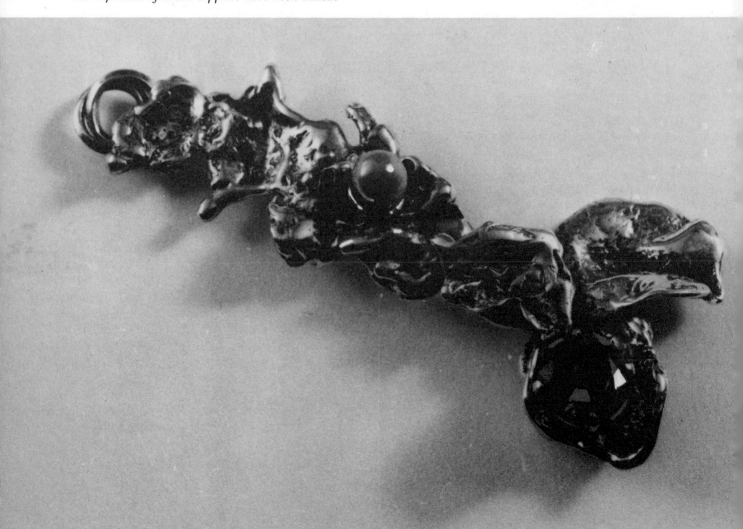

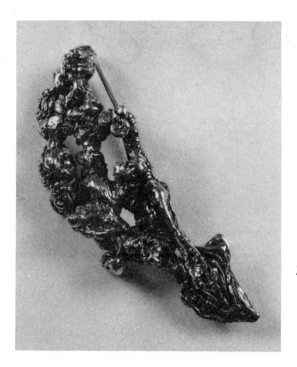

Figure 116. Centrifugally cast silver pin.

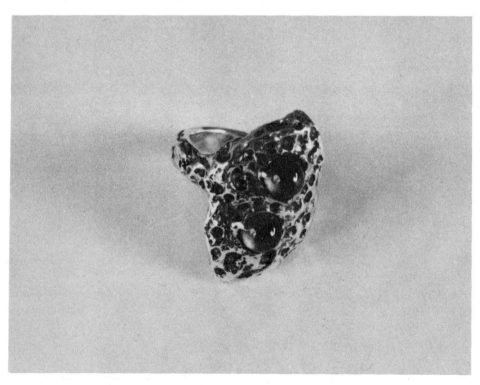

Figure 117. Centrifugally cast silver ring set with two amethyst cabochons.

Chapter Eleven

A WORD
ABOUT DESIGN

It is not our purpose to discuss or elaborate on the basic principles of design in general or of jewelry design in particular. There are scores of books that deal with these principles—shape, form, rhythm, balance, surface, color and a host of others. Our prime objective is to offer a word of encouragement to you, if you are one of those individuals who have a tendency to say, "I'm not an artist. I can't draw, so how can I design?" This, in the first place, may not be true. How do you know you cannot design if you have never tried? Secondly, the ability to design is not necessarily connected with the ability to draw or paint pictures. Thirdly, anybody can design anything—yes, anybody and anything! Whether it is a good or practical design for the object being designed can be another question. But who is to decide that? We might paraphrase the adage, "Beauty lies in the eyes of the beholder" to read, *"Good design* lies in the eyes of the beholder." And there have been any number of artists and artisans who have either ignored or violated the basic principles of art and/or design and yet have widely been heralded for the work they produced.

There have been people—jewelry craftsmen and members of the lay public—who have looked at our work and turned their noses up. There have been at least as many others who have looked and admired. Every artist and craftsman experiences this and learns to live with it. All this does not mean, however, that in terms of jewelry there are not certain fundamental rules that should be followed. Jewelry is meant to adorn the person who wears it. It should be so designed that it does this properly and without any discomfort to the wearer. Jewelry should also enhance the appearance of the wearer and not detract. Beyond that—when one gets down to the real nitty-gritty of jewelry design—there are actually few other restrictions. In the author's opinion, the steps to becoming a respectable designer-craftsman of jewelry—whether casting, fabrication or a combination of both methods is involved—are simply these:

1. Become proficient in the skills and techniques that are required. The best design ideas may never see the light of day unless you have mastered the how-to of making them happen. And all that requires is practice.

2. Know yourself. Think and decide what styles or mode of jewelry will best express you as an individual. Be your own severest critic in all you design and create. If you do not like anything you produce, be willing to cut it up and start again.

3. Study the jewelry that has been created in the past and that is currently being made, especially by professional craftsmen. Extract the best from what you see, but rather than be an imitator, use what attracted you and strike out in your own direction.

4. Striking out in your own direction means that you must be ready to experiment—not for the sake of experimenting, but for the purpose of inventing a new approach to the ideas that others have had before you. In short be an experimenter *and* inventor.

5. Believe that designs for jewelry are all around you—in a section of the paper on the wall, in a garden, in a partly or totally clouded sky, in a gnarled tree branch or even in its bark, in a weathered wood fence; in short, anywhere and everywhere. Be aware of every possibility, "seek and ye shall find"—especially in your own imagination.

Following are examples of the work of some widely recognized and highly regarded contemporary artist-craftsmen of jewelry. Although a very brief description is given of them and their achievements, the work resulting from their gifted minds and hands eloquently speaks for these master artisans.

CARRIE ADELL

Mrs. Adell started out as a highly trained and respected artist and has become a self-taught designer-craftsman of exceedingly beautiful jewelry. The products of her lively imagination and unique creativity have been exhibited in many museums, galleries, and craft shows on the Atlantic Seaboard. A member of the American Crafts Council and other professional organizations, she works in her home studio and has taught and still teaches jewelry crafting. She has won many honors for her work, not the least of which was the top award of the 1973 American Diamond Jewelry Competition for the bracelet shown. Her gold jewelry set with precious gemstones vividly communicates her distinctive individuality as an artist, experimenter and inventor.

Figure 118. Wedding bands. Each 14K yellow gold ring is composed of four sections, carved with different designs and assembled with 14-ga. wire rivets. Deep areas were sandblasted and high surfaces polished.

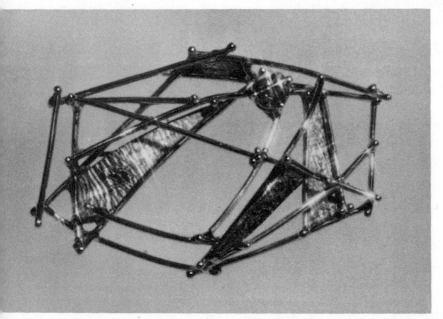

Figure 119. Pendant of 14K yellow gold set with ½-carat diamond. 22-ga. pink sheet wax textured and fused to 18-ga. wax wire.

Figure 120. Pendant constructed entirely of 16-ga. wax wire around clustered crystals of hessonite garnet (also called "cinnamon stone"). ¾-carat diamond is set in stamped prong box soldered to metal after casting and cleaning of piece.

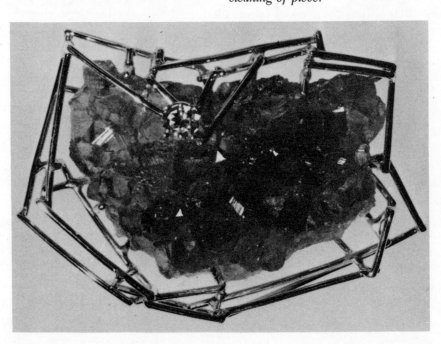

Figure 121. 30-in. chain. Oxydized beads made with red sticky wax trailed over 12-ga. wax wire to form erratic bridges. This piece was made into a mold so multiples could be made for future use in other chains.

Figure 122. Riveted bracelet with keyhole catch and safety on underside.
The assembly consisted of sawing sprues, filing and sanding,
adding three 14-ga. wire rivets and a 20-ga. wire figure-8 safety through the cast tubing,
polishing, and setting the 14 diamonds ranging from .10 to .02 points.

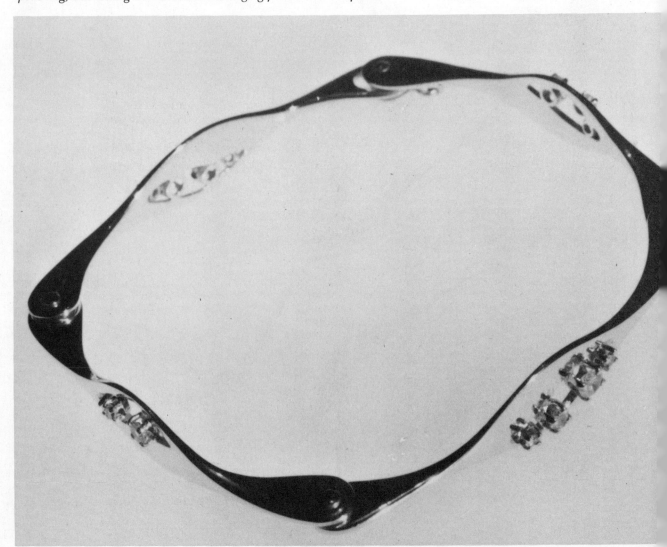

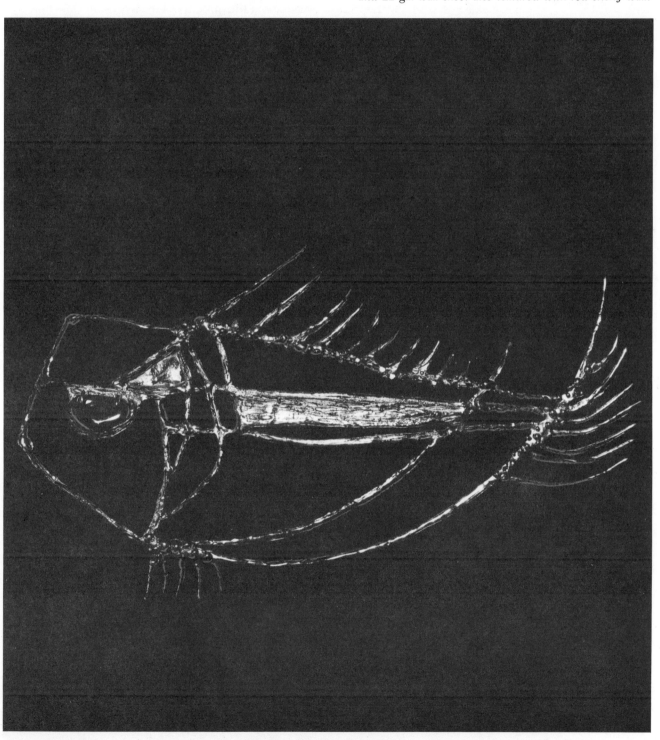

Figure 123. Fish pin with tumbled peridot eye.
Entirely built of 18-ga. wax wire upon which was trailed red sticky wax for texture,
and 22-ga. wax sheet also textured with red sticky wax.

Mr. Abramson is continuing a family tradition of three generations of excellent jewelry craftsmen. Having had a long career as artist, jewelry designer and craftsman, he is singularly trained to create distinguished one-of-a-kind jewelry. He has been accorded many honors and awards, and his work is not only exhibited in outstanding museums and galleries but also is sold in the finest jewelry establishments. He works in his home studio where he also teaches both wax-model-making for casting and jewelry fabrication. Illustrated are just a few examples of the very different and exquisitely handsome gold jewelry usually set with precious stones that Mr. Abramson designs and creates in his own individual idiom.

Figure 124. 14K gold ring set with three diamonds.

Figure 125. Cuff links are made of 14K gold, no stones.

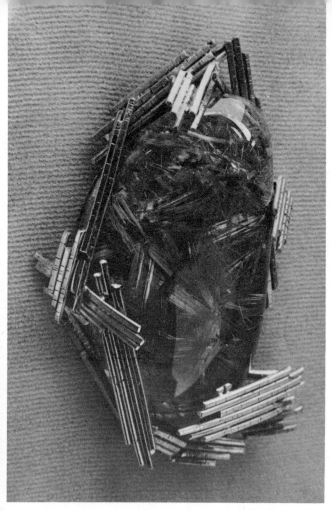

Figure 126. Pin or pendant of 14K gold with rutilated quartz. The stone used frequently gives the artist direction in terms of design.

Figure 127. Pin or pendant of 14K gold with two opals and six cultured pearls.

Figure 128.
14K gold ring,
no stones.

Figure 129.
14K gold ring.
The raised center circle
is made up of
a black onyx, a green onyx,
a sardonyx,
and a tigereye.

PAULA GOLLHARDT

Paula Gollhardt, a widely recognized and highly respected artisan of totally original jewelry, studied art at the University of Wisconsin and the Art Institute of Chicago. While she devotes a good deal of her time to the creation of body ornaments and other objects crafted in metal, she shares her enthusiasm for handcrafting jewelry by teaching adult as well as children's classes. The products of her gifted mind and talented hands have been displayed in galleries, museums and invitational craft shows from Boston to New York to Chicago and points between these great metropolitan centers. She currently is co-owner of a craft gallery, shop and school imaginatively called, "The Beautiful Things Factory, Inc." Her approach to the articles she fashions from precious metals and gemstones is bold in concept, and her designs combine what was good in the past with what is best in the contemporary mode.

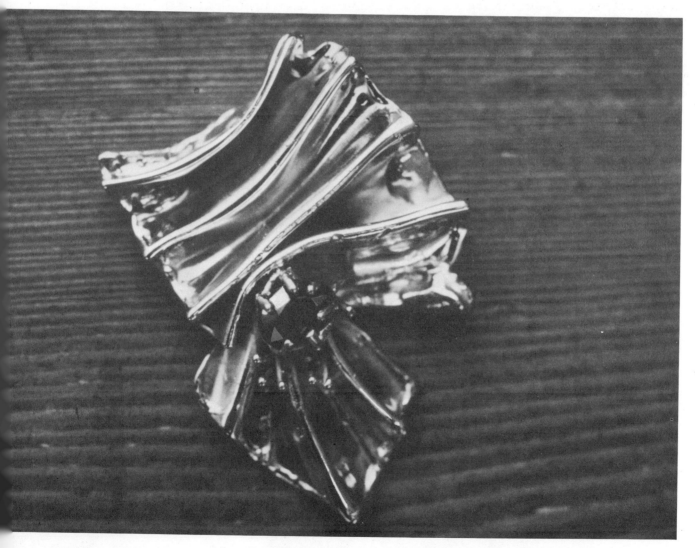

Figure 130. Cast 14K-gold pin, set with Madeira quartz.

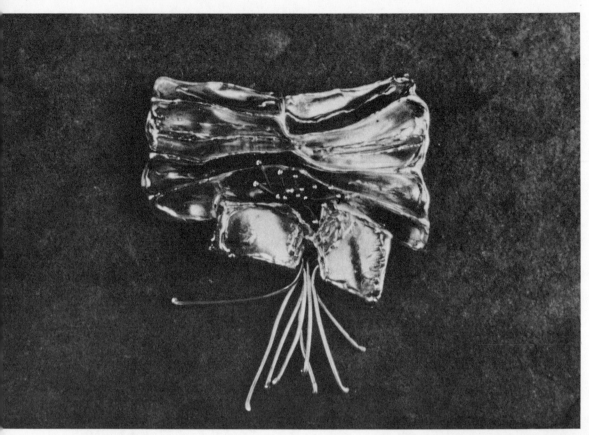

Figure 131. Pin/pendant,
cast sterling-silver
with fabricated dangling wires.

Figure 132.
Cast sterling-silver pin
with fabricated
14K-gold dangling wires.

Figure 133. Ring, cast sterling silver.

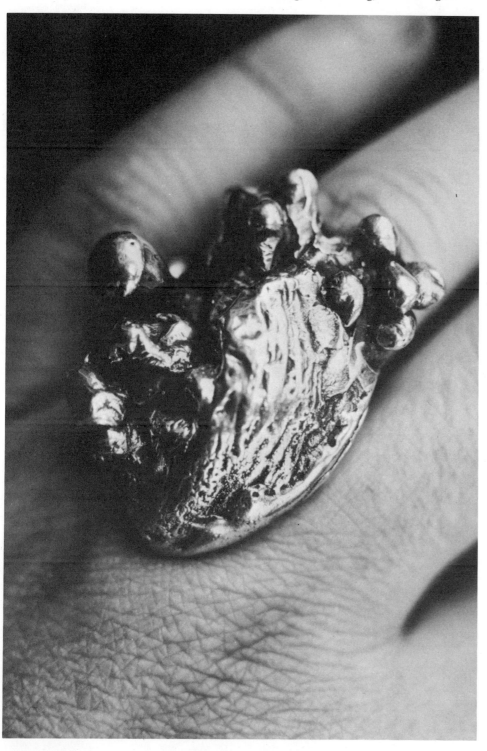

Figure 134. Pill box—constructed sterling-silver box and cover
with cast hollow-ball ornament soldered on cover.

Figure 135. Cast sterling-silver pin set with amethyst crystal.

Joseph Tartas, an Industrial Arts instructor at the secondary level, taught himself to design and handcraft jewelry almost thirty years ago. He has been casting jewelry by the lost wax process, however, for only a short time. Yet his work clearly displays the same mastery of that aspect of the field he earlier demonstrated in fabricated jewelry. He teaches jewelry making in adult classes and privately in his own workshop. He is active in many craft organizations, and has had the articles he designs and creates widely exhibited in craft shows, galleries and museums. He has won many awards—including, interestingly enough, a first prize in sculpture. His unique approach to jewelry and the novel methods he often employs for uniting unusual stones with precious metals are evident in these pictures of his work.

Figure 136. Four rings:
A. 14K yellow gold set with lapis lazuli.
B. Cast sterling silver set with tigereye.
C. Cast sterling silver.
D. Cast 14K green gold set with pyrite crystals.

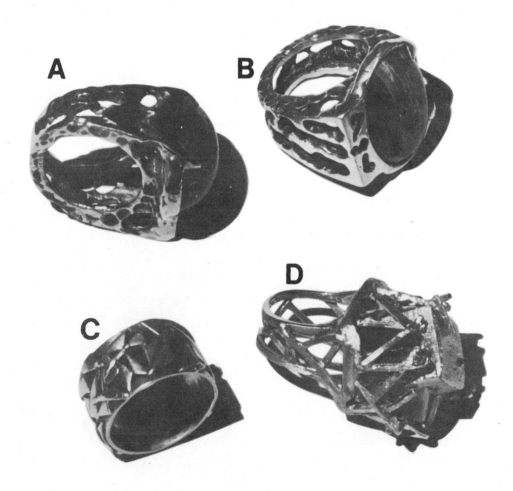

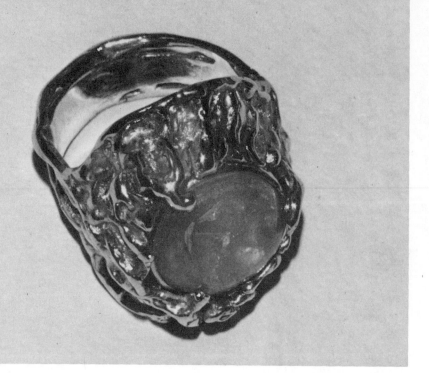

Figure 137.
Cast 14K yellow gold ring
set with opal.

Figure 138.
14K yellow gold pendant set
with Mexican fire opal
in matrix, fabricated chain.

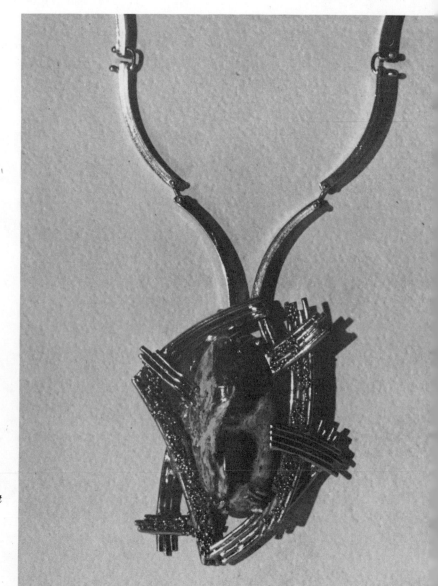

Figure 139. Pin, cast 14K
red gold set with
druse quartz.

Andre Sanchez apprenticed in jewelry design and creation in Barcelona, Spain, and reached the level of full modelmaker of carved wax articles cast in gold. His continued studies at the Escuela Masana in Spain further equipped him for positions as master jewelry designer in São Paulo, Brazil, and with such noteworthy New York City firms as David Webb, Carvin French Jewelry and others. His outstanding designs have been entered in many international competitions where he has been awarded a significant number of top honors. His creations have the touch of a fine sculptor as well as an accomplished jewelry artisan.

Figure 140.
Cast 14K gold pin/pendant.

Figure 141.
Pin/pendant, cast 14K gold.

Figure 142. Cast 14K gold ring.

Figure 143. Ring, cast 14K gold.

The jewelry pieces on this page and the next pages are the work of Maxine Antonsen, Bernard Raider, and Anthony Paol Ercio—all of whom are beginning students at the Abbey School of Jewelry and Art Metal Design in New York City.

Figure 144. Cast bronze pendant, by Maxine Antonsen.

Figure 145.
Cast bronze pendant
set with amethyst crystals
and turquoise,
by Maxine Antonsen

Figure 146.
Cast sterling-silver pendant
set with large
labradorite and faceted
semiprecious stones,
by Maxine Antonsen.

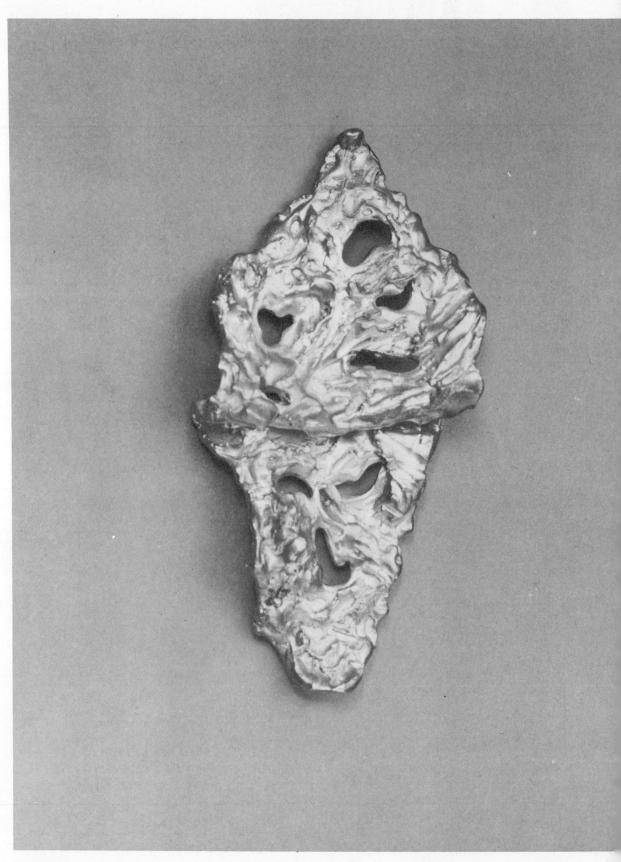

*Figure 147. Pin, cast manganese bronze alloyed with 10 per cent
sterling silver, by Bernard Raider.*

Figure 148.
Cast sterling-silver ring,
by Anthony Paol Ercio.

Figure 149.
Ring, cast sterling silver,
by Anthony Paol Ercio.

SOURCES OF SUPPLY

Abbey Materials Corp.
116 West 29th Street
New York, N.Y. 10001

AKG & Company
1114 Greentree Road
Newark, Del. 19711

(Mail Order)
Allcraft Tool & Supply Company,
   Inc.
215 Park Avenue
Hicksville, N.Y. 11801

(Salesroom)
Allcraft Tool & Supply Company,
   Inc.
22 West 48th Street
New York, N.Y. 10036

Alpha Faceting Supply
Box 2133
Bremerton, Wash. 98310

Anchor Tool & Supply Co., Inc.
12 John Street
New York, N.Y. 10036

Barnard's
4724 Broadway
Kansas City, Missouri 64112

Baskin & Sons, Inc.
732 Union Ave.
Middlesex, N.J. 08846

Bourget Bros.
1626 11th Street
Santa Monica, Calif. 90404

California Casting Supply, Inc.
2084 E. Foothill Blvd.
Pasadena, Calif. 91104

California Crafts Supply
1096 North Main Street
Orange, Calif. 92667

Casting Supply House, Inc.
62 West 47th Street
New York, N.Y. 10036

Craftool Company, Inc.
1421 W. 240th Street
Harbor City, Calif. 90710

William Dixon Company
Carlstadt, N.J. 07072

Dick Ells Co.
908 Venice Blvd.
Los Angeles, Calif. 90015

Five M Gems
270 East 17th St.
Costa Mesa, Calif. 92627

Greigers, Inc.
900 S. Arroyo Parkway
Pasadena, Calif. 91109

T. B. Hagstoz & Son
709 Sansom St.
Philadelphia, Pa. 19106

C. R. Hill Co.
35 W. Grand River Ave.
Detroit, Mich. 48226

B. Jadow and Sons, Inc.
53 West 23rd St.
New York, N.Y. 10010

Jeweler Aids Company
130-40 227th St.
Laurelton, N.Y. 11413

Kerr Sybron Corp.
Dept. L
28200 Wick Road
Romulus, Mich. 48174

Lapidabrade, Inc.
8 East Eagle Road
Havertown, Pa. 19083

Lapidary Center
4114 Judah Street
San Francisco, Calif. 94122

Maroon Bells Industries, Inc.
3400 Tejon St.
Denver, Colo. 80211

Minnesota Lapidary Supply
524 North 5th St.
Minneapolis, Minn. 55401

Montana Assay Office
610 S.W. 2nd Ave.
Portland, Ore. 97204

O'Brien's
1116 N. Wilcox Ave.
Hollywood, Calif. 90038

Redondo Gems & Mineral Co.
1315 Aviation Blvd.
Redondo Beach, Calif. 90278

Rochester Lapidary Supply Co.
P.O. Box 6350
Highway 63, North
Rochester, Minnesota 55901

Romanoff Rubber Co., Inc.
153-159 W. 27th St.
New York, N.Y. 10001

Swenson's Lapidary Equipment
9641 E. Apache Trail
Mesa, Ariz. 85207

Swest Inc.
P.O. Box 1298
118 Broadway
San Antonio, Texas 78295
OR
P.O. Box 2010
1712 Jackson
Dallas, Texas 75221

Technical Specialties International,
Inc.
487 Elliot Avenue West
Seattle, Wash. 98119

Technicraft Lapidaries Corp.
2248 Broadway
New York, N.Y. 10024

U.S. Lapidary Supply Co., Inc.
1605 W. San Carlos St.
San Jose, Calif. 95128

Zymex
900 W. Los Vallecitos Blvd.
San Marcos, Calif. 92069

INDEX